P9-CRV-616

Praise for *Prayers for People Who Say They Can't Pray*

"Donna Schaper has collected the prayers we didn't know existed and written the ones we didn't know we needed. Prayer? You can do this."

—Lillian Daniel, author *When "Spiritual But Not Religious" Is Not Enough*

"Every breath with intention is prayer. You are already praying, and what's showing up in your life are their answers. Don't like what you see? Walk and pray yourself in a new direction."

—Ron Buford, founder, God is Still Speaking in the United Church of Christ

"Schaper has successfully introduced 'DIY prayers' and assured us that prayer belongs in all of our lives. I loved the book not only for Schaper's wisdom about prayers but also for her writing and candid sharing of her own life and those moments that challenged her and taught her lessons."

—Marrianna Houston, writer, international humanitarian

"Unpredictable, surprising, and always worth reading, Donna Schaper is one of those unusual writers who helps us with her wisdom and with her deep understanding of what life is. She even helps us pray."

—Esther Cohen, poet, writer, storyteller, book doctor

"A real need met by a real writer, who knows prayer and the people who think they can't pray."

—Bishop Spong, author and retired bishop

"Let Donna Schaper put words in your mouth, and you won't regret it. Let her put words in your heart, and you'll never be the same."

—Quinn G. Caldwell, author of *All I Really Want*

PRAYERS FOR PEOPLE WHO SAY THEY CAN'T

PRAY

DONNA SCHAPER

Abingdon Press

Nashville

PRAYERS FOR PEOPLE WHO SAY THEY CAN'T PRAY

Copyright © 2014 by Donna Schaper

All rights reserved.
No part of this work may be reproduced or transmitted in any form or
by any means, electronic or mechanical, including photocopying and re-
cording, or by any information storage or retrieval system, except as may
be expressly permitted by the 1976 Copyright Act or in writing from the
publisher. Requests for permission can be addressed to Permissions, The
United Methodist Publishing House, P.O. Box 801, 201 Eighth Avenue
South, Nashville, TN 37202-0801, or e-mailed to permissions@umpub
lishing.org.

Library of Congress Cataloging-in-Publication Data

Schaper, Donna.
    Prayers for people who say they can't pray / Donna Schaper.
        pages cm.
    ISBN 978-1-4267-8869-7
    1. Prayers.   I. Title.
    BL560.S33 2014
    242'.8—dc23

                                                                2014028599

Scripture quotations unless noted otherwise are taken from the Common English Bible. Copyright © 2011 by the Common English Bible. All
rights reserved. Used by permission. www.CommonEnglishBible.com.

Scripture quotations marked KJV are taken from The Authorized (King
James) Version. Rights in the Authorized Version in the United Kingdom
are vested in the Crown. Reproduced by permission of the Crown's pat-
entee, Cambridge University Press.

14 15 16 17 18 19 20 21 22 23—10 9 8 7 6 5 4 3 2 1
MANUFACTURED IN THE UNITED STATES OF AMERICA

CONTENTS

Introduction
Prayers for People Who Maybe Believe | vii

Chapter One:
Ordinary Prayers When Waking, When Sleeping | 1

Chapter Two:
Prayers for Those Who Are Too Busy to Pray | 15

Chapter Three:
Prayers to Calm the Monkey's Mind | 31

Chapter Four:
Prayers for the Great Recession to Recede | 49

Chapter Five:
Road-Strengthening Prayers for the Commuting Soul | 69

Chapter Six:
Prayers for the Broken Heart | 85

Chapter Seven:
When Hurt, Ill, or Lost | 99

Chapter Eight:
For That Which Is Other to Us | 119

Chapter Nine:
Prayers for Hatching, Matching, and Dispatching | 141

Chapter Ten:
Prayers Through the Months and Seasons | 165

Afterword:
Where to Start: On Writing Your Own Prayers | 185

Prayers for People
Who Maybe Believe

THIS COLLECTION OF PRAYERS offers comfort, exclamation, praise, groan, and lament for believers, unbelievers, wanna-be believers, and might-have-been believers. To pray when you are not sure what you believe is to honor your uncertainty; it is to take your doubt or ambivalence or desire or anger seriously enough to turn all that emotion and thought into prayer. It assures us all in our many parts and many moods that everything is going to be OK, despite mounting evidence to the contrary.

Some of these prayers end with the old-fashioned word *Amen*. Others do not. Some of them are crafted to be offered by an individual, others by a group (although, of course, you could adapt them). Some of them echo tradition. Others break from tradition. These prayers try to go to the edge of what we know as prayer and forge a new path.

When we pray as people who kind of believe and sort of don't, when we pray as ordinary people, we make the tentative a high art. By tentative I mean what ancient people meant by a tent, a place of shelter along a long journey. I also mean the tentative as the might be or may have been or could be. Tentative means a tendency to hope and lean forward, gladly, knowing we are sheltered on our way by something larger than ourselves.

Of course solid people, the kind with spiritual homes and not just spiritual tents, can pray solid prayers. Many cannot. Many don't have a spiritual or religious cradle, much less a grown-up spiritual home. Cradle Christians like me have a head start on solid or memorized or ancient prayers. But many people did not go to Head Start spiritually or even to half-day spiritual kindergarten. In their name, this book is written. As for those of us who grew up learning the ancient prayers, sometimes those prayers still seem to serve, and sometimes they feel worn-out. This book is written in the name of those people, too, those people who know the old prayers but sometimes find themselves needing new ones. In fact, when we know the old prayers by heart, we often enjoy reading and writing new ones especially.

Our capacity for wonder is awakened when there is a continuation of the traditions of prayer that we love.

Both believers and unbelievers and halfway interested people can use this book to formulate honest, tentative prayers that come from the gut. When prayer is genuine, we pray from our guts and not just from our heads. Our heads don't go away. Instead, our hearts and hopes join them. Some people believe in God—or assent to God's possible existence—but are mad with God. How can God let innocent children suffer or my ennui continue? Something happened to them, and their belief went straight to their head, without their heart following. Still others are disappointed by God's answers to their prayers. This book contains disappointment and anger with God.

When people say, "I don't know how to pray," what they often mean is "I don't believe." When people say, "I don't believe," they often mean a larger and more difficult disappointment. They mean *I tried and I'm not going to try any more, at least for now*. They also mean that they can't trust.

This book is written to remove obstacles to prayer and to show how honest prayer doesn't require belief or trust or constant satisfaction. Sometimes our heart has a wisdom that our head does not. A voice in our head might be telling us that prayer is a waste of time, but some other part of our soul yearns to pray.

Sometimes prayer comes from our bodies—and that is a good, true thing. We fold our hands or we bow down. Or we experience terror or gratitude or find ourselves with tears in our eyes. These tears can be gladness and relief or sorrow and remorse. Prayer has intellectual power and nuance, but prayer also needs an involved and connected belly to be authentic.

When I was six, my father beat up my mother so badly that I had to call the police. He did that a lot. One night, something in me broke open, and I dialed 911, a number that somehow I knew but did not know that I knew. After I called the police, I called my pastor, Pastor Witte. He came. He was able to calm my father down, for then. Since that day I have had a warm spot in my stomach that confuses Pastor Witte with God. I have dedicated my life to keeping children safe. I count on someone, like God, to answer. Do I know there is a God on the other end of the line? No. Still, I dial. When I speak to people about God, I speak from my stomach, from that warm confidence that abides, despite lots of good reasons for it to go out of existence or on to a shelf. Why do I, a believer—in fact, a pastor—write prayers for those who may not or cannot believe? Because I know God rarely answers prayers. That may shock you, but I think it is true.

Because I am aware of how many children call on the name of God for a slice of bread or an ounce of protection and no God comes. God's record is not good. I trust in the God my belly knows. There is persistent warmth in my stomach. But I am also deeply disappointed by all the stories I have heard about a busy signal on the line. The need for this book is the distance many people experience from God. Perhaps it is that the word *God* or the word *believe* got too big. Perhaps there is an aspect of God that is distant. Whatever the reason, these prayers bridge the gap between the distant God and you. You don't have to believe in God to experience comfort. You don't have to buy the whole package to get a little assurance from the sacred. Neither prayer nor pastors stop domestic violence or child abuse—but they help us get through such experiences. Prayer tells us "it's going to be OK," even when we pay for the gas that costs more than we have and we have apocalyptic thoughts.

There is a cultural chaos around time—a loss of rhythm, a loss of calendar. We no longer know how to structure our days, perhaps because the Internet is open 24-7 or because our culture has broken down into too many moving parts. Many of us wake up to turn on a machine and go to sleep turning off a machine. We might instead pray our way awake or pray our way to sleep. This book will show you how. When folk culture breaks down, we forget how to hatch, match, and dispatch. We forget how to order our relationships and our lives. This book helps us find ways to ritualize rites of passage without going back to the "stone age."

When we say things we really do mean—like stop the violence against my mother and my planet—to deities who may or may not exist, we focus our inner lives. We make the inner active. When we wake to gratitude and sleep to remembrance of the day, we focus our inner lives. When we have rites of passage all along the way, we focus our inner lives in both the Holy and our communities. We also become strong for the world and what it throws at us. Prayer may be a reorientation of our interior lives, but it also resources what we have to do on the road, at the job, and in the kitchen.

Prayer is a decision to move out of time on behalf of time. "Lord give me patience and make it snappy," says one self-mocking person who is trying to pray. This good joke about prayer joins my other favorite misunderstanding of prayer, which happened while standing at the bedside of a dying patient. I asked if she would mind if I prayed. She said, "No, not at all, if it helps you." Prayer has a habit of being misunderstood. It is more for us than for God.

Prayer finds the quiet corner in the loud party and there

looks and listens. It tunes in to find out what it is we want, feel, desire, and think. It is like a poem, which Robert Frost describes as a momentary stay against confusion.

I remember vividly one pastoral experience that involved me flying in a helicopter to Massachusetts General Hospital from Amherst after a nine-year-old boy had been hit in the head by a baseball bat. He was unconscious and being airlifted. His father and I watched his eyes descend farther into his head as we sped over the summer trees. "The God I don't believe in, Donna, is right here, right now, with us, right?" "Yes," I said, only half believing it myself.

Carl Jung—who thought we smuggled our biography into everything—kept a solid bronze plaque on the wall outside his office in Zurich that said, "Bidden or Not Bidden, God is Present." (*Vocatus Atque Non Vocatus Deus Aderit.*) I don't completely agree. I think that is possible but not certain. My prayers here are not sneaky ways to get you to recognize God. My goal is to recognize the experiences that evoke the language, "Oh, my God." A car accident evokes an "Oh, my God" horror that is comparable to the awe when we see a great sunset. When we say these three words, we are already praying. Because we misunderstand prayer as the property of believers, we call our language "just" an exclamation. Some fundamentalists whose theology is not actually fundamental, but punishing, have exacerbated this misunderstanding of prayer as a way of self-righteously manipulating a self-righteous God. They give prayer a bad name. Instead, exclamation goes to the heart of human experience, and prayer provides a momentary stay against the confusion of that experience.

I had a writing teacher once who said that his students only got seven exclamation points a year. Maybe we should have a prayer allotment as well. But most of us would overspend that account: there is much that is both beautiful and ugly that requires exclamation points.

Prayers beckon exclamation points. They enchant us. They let us shiver with grace. We realize that the many times we say "Oh, my God!" we are sort of praying to a God we sort of imagine is out there.

Other cultures would argue that "OM" is a primordial sound, almost a grunt that acknowledges a mystery way beyond any need to believe in it. Prayer is often more sound than words, more chant than songs, and more instrumental than vocal. A signed benediction for the deaf can often be more useful to those with ears that can hear. Humming a hymn we sort of remember can be a kind of prayer as well. With apologies to the beauty of silence, I offer these words and prayers.

Prayer is not the capturing of God for our own needs. Whenever I am asked to pray in public, I say, "God who is beyond any name by which we imprison you, God whom some know as Spirit, others as Jesus, others as Christ, others as Yahweh, or Ruach, or Breath, still others as Allah, yet others as Force or Divine, release us from the foolishness of thinking we know your name." That utter humility is the starting place of any prayer. It starts when we acknowledge that we don't know God and yet need someone to talk to who is not human, who is human plus, or human other. Prayer is a human leaning towards the edge. It happens when we are thrust to the edge of what we know. Prayer is a human in full-tilt boogie awareness that there is more to life than itself. Prayer happens in the "Oh, my God" statement we make when we stand at the limit of what we understand and still have the audacity to speak or at least groan in a primitive kind of communication with ourselves at the edge of ourselves.

I pray therefore to a God whom I am pretty sure is not Pastor Witte, nor Lutheran nor my current (United Church of Christ) denomination's snapshot of the cosmos. I see both Pastor Witte's success and failure. I am also not convinced that my husband's Judaism has the right picture of God, though some of Judaism's ways of imaging God deeply move me. I *am* sure that the certainty of the pilots on 9/11 is not of God. I am unimpressed with most monotheists and all triumphalists. I have more certainty about who God is not than about who God is.

I write prayers for people who are tentative about God because I trust in the human being's capacity to ask for a partner. I trust in the human's capacity to need, exclaim, articulate, and focus. I trust in the groan. I trust in the enchantment. I know disenchantment reigns: but prayer, perhaps, can re-enchant those who are disenchanted. Prayer is not just the need for help; it is also the understanding of beauty. The real polarity in life is not that between the sacred and the profane: it is the quarrel between the sacred and the desecrated, de-sacralized flatness. Prayer re-enchants by noting the many levels, the densities of our existence.

I offer these prayers as momentary stays against confusion, as poems, as pictures of what we might say if we were to speak our heart's deepest longings, and if we were to find a way to trust the universe and its partnership with you and me.

CHAPTER ONE

Ordinary Prayers When Waking, When Sleeping

P RAYER CAN TURN AN ORDINARY DAY into an extraordinary one. Einstein said there are two ways to understand life: first, that nothing is a miracle, or second, that everything is a miracle. The prayers here sense the sacred in the ordinary. They believe that everything is a miracle, if we but give it the consciousness it deserves.

I remember the way I went to sleep as a child. Pastor Witte had taught me to pray. His instruction was less an invitation than a command. "This is what you should do when you go to sleep." *Should* was a big word in the religion of my youth, and it rarely occurred to me to question it. I just did what I was told. I am no longer able to be religious or spiritual in that way. Thus I reach for ways to pray beyond the *should*.

1

But first, the old way. On the way to sleep I was to mention everyone I loved and name him or her by name: Mom, Dad, Grandma, Grandpa, Papa Ike (our borrowed grandfather), Cathy (my sister), Jesse (my brother), assorted aunts and uncles. As an innovation on the ritual I also prayed for my cats and dog. Pastor Witte didn't mind, nor did he ever know.

When I woke up, I was to give thanks for the opportunities and challenges of the day. I was encouraged to wake slowly and sleep slowly, giving time to a ritual of preparation and benediction. I didn't even know the word ritual then. But still I had one. I had a way to lie down and a way to get up. It involved prayer.

Back in those days, in a small river town on the Hudson, I also had a glow-in-the-dark cross. As soon as the light faded, it ignited with light. The darker the better was its motto. The cross was as plastic as plastic could be, but there it was—shining—if I woke up in the night. That plastic cross managed my dreams and my nightmares, just by being there, in the same way that the prayers managed the obligation I felt to others. The morning prayers were simpler than the evening ones. "Thank you for my school. Thank you for my ice skates. Thank you for breakfast." They went quicker because the usual day had only two or three things happening at any given time, unless it was a holiday, when thanksgiving was appropriate for jelly-filled cookies. If I had three cents in my pocket, which I did every now and then, there might be the jelly donut on the way to school. Prayers for jelly appear to have been featured.

I also had childish pictures on my wall, in the lower bunk bed. A waterfall. Some words from the teacher. I had a ritualized life. Now I do not: I live in airports, hotels, my country place, and my city place. I wish I still had a night-light to carry along to my multiple-choice beds. Or if not a plastic cross, then at least a pattern to my peripatetic being. I long for the patterns as much as the prayers.

What has replaced my ritual is a longing for ritual. But, I do have a few. I light a candle when I start my morning writing. I insist on prayers whenever I eat, wherever I eat. I carry a coffee cup around and refill it. I don't know how I stopped the childhood practice of prayer on the way to sleep and prayer on the way to waking. I do know that it stopped, and that I found other ways to stand on the threshold of my time.

During that long period of having children at home, mostly when my head hit the pillow, I went to sleep. Waking up usually had to do with someone in a wet diaper jumping on my belly, wondering what was for breakfast or if they could turn on *Sesame Street*.

Now in the empty nest, if not the empty next, the cell phone has become a bit of a ritual. I use it as an alarm clock and as a good morning, picking it up to see what I missed while sleeping.

I can justify the cell phone ritual. But I don't think Pastor Witte would approve. I am interested in what is going to happen next. I am overly concerned about my grown children and wonder if they will have e-mailed or texted while I was dreaming.

My husband and I do have a morning ritual, which is a snuggle. It makes me very happy and is surely close to prayer in its power. But I practice a new version of the old *should*. I practice it before I pick up the cell phone on a good day. It resembles the pattern of yore: at night give thanks for those you love. In the morning give thanks for what you are looking forward to during the day. Find at least three things and name them: coffee with a friend, dinner at home, and strength to make a hard phone call. These "forward lookings" or "long thinkings" give prayer an anticipatory pattern. The morning prayers help to name thanksgiving for what is to come.

In Jewish practice there is a mezuzah on the front door. On your way out of the house, you touch it, giving thanks for your home. On your way in, you touch it, giving thanks for a safe return to the place you call home. In my childhood practice and with the mezuzah, there is a great sense of threshold, a sense of God as guarding our "goings out and our comings in."

I have a friend whose ancient African American grandmother told him to wake up and check out the news. Why? "Let's find out what they done to us overnight." She was praying but in a terrified way or at least a way to mitigate terror. She taught her grandson a morning ritual.

I offer these prayers as a mezuzah, a way to guard the thresholds of nights and mornings. You may want to follow Pastor Witte's instructions. They do help sleep along. You may, upon rising, want to answer the question, "What are you looking forward to today?" You might even want to acknowledge dread: "What do you fear today?" Rituals that guard our goings out and our comings in are important.

Everybody has a night and a morning, whether you are a poet, a racist, or a prisoner. Saying yes to others at night and to self in the morning is a good way to pray.

❖

When I wake up in the morning, let my first thought be gladness to be alive. Let me slow into the waking and wake to a long slow day. Keep that cell phone and computer close by, but let them not be in charge. And if I can't pray before I touch a button, let me pray right after I've checked out the world's wide web. **Amen.**

Let me remember those I love, by name, even if they are far away or no longer close in spirit. Or let me announce my excitement and dread for the day, in such a way that I stare straight at them with spirit and with power. Let me not just act but also reflect my way to action. Let me ritualize my rising and begin my own days my own way. And when I am slowly ready and slowly awake and genuinely ritualized, let me rise. **Amen.**

Holy Spirit, you are a kind of dailiness that makes the ordinary extraordinary. How do we solve a problem twice our size? Bite off a piece of it every day. Chew it. Enjoy it. Resolve it. Be done with it and move on. That's how. Show us how to live the way you live, one holy step at a time. And dedicate this little bit of my self and my day to the complete coming of your entire realm. **Amen.**

When I go to sleep at night, let me name those I love and say thank you to them again for being alive. Let my goings out and my comings in have a bit of pizzazz, O God. Let me be a person with rituals: a mezuzah to touch, a keychain to treasure, a long walk home on a nice night. Let my stopping and starting aim somewhere. And keep chaos at bay. **Amen.**

Thoreau wanted to live deliberately the way that I want to be fully awake. Deliberately awake. That is my goal. Is it all right if I meet the goal slightly, every few days? Or is something more complete demanded of me? **Amen.**

Tranquility: what the heck is that? I have a feeling someone somewhere knows what it is. I'd love to find out. Can you teach me, O God, or must I be my own teacher? **Amen.**

When I ask for transformation from a monkey mind, one that jumps from tree to tree and subject to subject, I am not asking for pamper camp, as though I were still a baby. I am asking for a discipline, not from the outside, but from the inside. Let me be a person who can focus on one thing at a time and is in charge of myself. **Amen.**

When I listen to the whispered longing of my own heart in my own ear, I hear my heartbeat for justice and fairness, my soul crying out for liberty and joy. Give me permission to really feel and want these things today, yesterday and tomorrow. Thank you. **Amen.**

William Butler Yeats argued that we can "live with a clearer, perhaps even with a fiercer life because of our quiet." Grant me ferocity, clarity, and quiet. **Amen.**

Help me to pray for all the towns and cities in which I have lived. Let me start with the first one, where I was born, and enjoy it street by street. Let this be a long project and a long prayer. Don't rush my memory. **Amen.**

You promise, O God, prophets and seers. You promise a cold cup of water to the straggler on a hot summer day. You promise that we can lose to gain and have what we can let go of. I thank you for your promises. **Amen.**

For a little peace, a little purpose, and a lot of satisfaction, I pray. Guarantee that I rise with vigor and retire with grace, and not just today but in a way that teases eternity with my presence. **Amen.**

My prayers are such small boats, such little bridges. The ocean is vast, the world enormous. I stand in awe at the small chance to be a small part of it. I consider my e-mail address and the World Wide Web and stand amazed at where I can go and who I can be. Let me be at home in my small home and in your large world. **Amen.**

Wake me up with your beauty, O God. Let me see you wherever you are. Let me tell you just how good you look to me. **Amen.**

For a way to sing a strange song in a strange land, and not to care who is listening, I pray. Put all my regrets in a pile every day and let me find a way to live past them into what's left of the future that has not been stolen by the past. **Amen.**

Help me define why I am here, O God, and then walk with me towards that future. Aim me with an aim that is worthy of you and me. **Amen.**

Grant me the confidence to see through and to the other side of betrayal. Let me pay attention to my part in it and find a way to either cease and desist or at least gain forgiveness. When I can't get to the other side of betrayal, find someone to stand with me, right where I am, and to retain hope in the other side. **Amen.**

Parent us, O God, and let us know where we come from and to whom we truly belong. Let us find a way to thank our parents today, whether they are dead or alive. **Amen.**

Train our muscles, O God, to see the truth and to love it. Teach us to recover and then to move again. When I go to the gym, let me exercise all of my parts. **Amen.**

Help me get better at finding the questions at the heart of most answers, the beginnings inside most endings. **Amen.**

Timeless God who became time in Jesus, draw near and rest our alarms. Let them go off at the right times, to you. And also, if it pleases you, let us rest. **Amen.**

Gifts mount in us, but all we can manage is a few dollars in the plate. Let us erupt into time and space like a volcano of giftedness—and please accept our overflowing selves as an offering. We know that we have riches to squander. Let us squander some toward you. **Amen.**

Surely, our days are numbered—by birth, baptism, confirmation, marriage, death, and all the birthdays in between. Surely, our breaths are numbered by what moments we allow ourselves breathtaking experiences. Thanks be to you, Great Numberer, for the days we have. **Amen.**

Gloom we always have with us. Joy requires tending. Tend in us joy—and let us tend it in others. Dispense the gloom easily and puff it away, then breathe in the joy. We know what money can't buy. It can't buy us love, and it can't buy us joy, and we want both. Empty us so that we can be filled with good things. Let nothing be wasted on us. **Amen.**

The best revenge is not to become like the one whom you hate for hurting you. Marcus Aurelius and Nietzsche both said the same thing another way: Let me not become the monster I am destroying in you. Let there be no need to destroy in me. Instead, let me be a great collector of life, one who fills out what is missing by imagination and forgiveness. **Amen.**

Let me pick up one stone today. One that no one else has yet touched. Let me love it. Let me touch the stone with a warm hand and steal the cold from it. Open my heart to a new generosity, a melted insecurity, and a warm hand that refuses to go cold on life.

"The best time to plant a tree is yesterday," says a wild old saying. Johnny Appleseed is celebrated as a great man. Why? He gave something to life that would outlast him. He followed that great Boy Scout dictum that advises us to make one improvement on life before we exit. Spiritual gleaners glean the future as well as the past. Teach me how to glean. **Amen.**

CHAPTER TWO

Prayers for Those
Who Are Too Busy to Pray

H OW CAN YOU BE TOO BUSY? Too busy to exercise? Too busy to pray? What are we saying when we say we are too busy?

My favorite book is *A Pattern Language: Towns, Buildings, Construction*. Published in 1977 by Oxford University Press, for architects and designers, it lays out a Western version of Feng Shui. What is around us matters. If a house has a window seat in it, that will matter to the psychology, spirituality, and freedom of the inhabitants. If a room has more than one window, we will enjoy the room more. We will make the room "roomy." We will inhabit the space.

What a wonderful word, *inhabitant*. The one who dwells there, habits there, and makes ritual there.

If we spend all day in a windowless room, the lack of spaciousness and openness will hurt our spirits. We will find ourselves in a narrow way, which is the Hebrew notion of sin. When we live in the narrow way, it is like sin. Sin is distance from God. It is the refusal to maximize our human potential. It is also to miss the mark of our living and to become as Martin Luther said, "*Incurvatus in Se*." *Curved in on ourselves* is the translation. When we live in a room with windows, we pattern ourselves out of sin. We are not sinless but on our way out of sin, getting closer to God, closer to our true selves and releasing that terrible curve of the spine and the hurt which turns in on itself and consumes itself.

Many of us have become patterned to discomfort. We imagine the commute will be rough. *Traffic*, we say, *what else is new?* We imagine with annoyance that there will be a Starbucks and a Subway on every corner—and guess what, there is. Oddly, time explodes while space conforms to a certain sameness. Prayer helps us take time out of chaos and even to see space with more diversity. It gives us a beauty to comfort us while we also live in the ugliness surrounding.

Prayer interrogates what we mean by being too busy. Too busy for what? Who is inhabiting our time and space if not us? Who is telling us what to do with our time? Have we been invaded by outer space or by aliens? I can name some of the aliens, those who alienate us. They are our to-do lists, our jobs, our patterns of living without patterns. The aliens are a cultural economy to which we assent. We are to work longer, harder. We are to succeed. We are to consume. We are to get to the top of the pile or at least take our children to tutoring so they will get high test scores so they won't be at the bottom of the pile. We know our marching orders. They do not include prayer because no one is going to pay us to pray. That being said, prayer locates the inner space that can conquer the invasion by the outer space aliens. Prayer asks us to ask questions and to become people who live in their own homes, in their own patterns, and who know how to open their windows and look around.

I know it is unpopular to say anything but "I'm too busy." Keeping a Sabbath is practically a crime. It may mean that you are slothful or not working hard enough. You already accept responsibility for debt, forgetting that great line in the Lord's Prayer about forgiving our debts as we forgive the debts of others. If you don't have a job or are poor, surely it is your fault. It couldn't possibly be the "fault" of a cultural economy that loves to tell people that they are too busy, while making people too busy, and then blaming them for their own business in a contorted way.

Prayer challenges the cultural economy at its base. It says that being is as good as doing. It says that inner space is a good alternative to outer space. Note that wonderful word "alternative." It means alter (which is the Latin for "other") narrative. When we say we are too busy, we go along with the commanding narrative. We are actually bragging about how we participate in our own oppression. When we say we're not too busy to pray, we move into that room called alternative. There the windows open and let us see.

Deliver us from the hypocrisy of sounding reasonable while being unreasonable, from defending our own anxieties instead of our own hopes. Deliver us from the fiction that we don't have enough time and drive us to the meaning of that claim. Yes, we will die. Yes, we may live before we die. We have the time we have. Let us be glad in it. Let a little depth enter our fear that we don't have enough time. **Amen.**

Deliver us from our internal daily scolding and allow our own words to our selves be liberating. Yes, you have the time you have. Yes, you love the time you have. Yes, it is enough. **Amen.**

Teach us to understand the time famine and the trust famine and move us to be leaders in a time feast and a trust feast. Help us alert others that we have enough time and that our time is our own. Let us trust others and lead the bandwagon toward more trust, by being trustworthy. When our friends tell us they are too busy to see us, let us not applaud them but instead gently chide them. **Amen.**

When we wonder how we'll ever get things done, and we find ourselves folding our husband's laundry, after he has folded ours the last time, let us touch his clothes with joy that we know him, gladness in his T-shirts, happiness that we have this task. Let us learn how to do mundane tasks with magnificence. **Amen.**

When we realize we are under water and that our house is a mess, drive us to the meaning of these metaphors. Help us see that we are flooded with pressures, scattered, and tossed about. Let us avoid denial about the sense of drowning and help us to learn to swim. When we are as piled up as our junk mail is on the counter, release us to some kind of order, even if it is a big paper bag that fills up with what we no longer want nor can manage. Help us de-clutter so that we may re-clutter with more style. Help us work on the fear issues as well as the clutter and from there to bring spirit to ordinary living. Tomorrow let us awake to fearlessness in the face of the mail and the e-mail, the water level and the house. **Amen.**

When stuck in traffic or stuck in emotional traffic or stuck in a fellow worker's refusal to get back to us on e-mail, teach us to chant or sing or hum. Let us not let the most inefficient person or thing in our world drive us. Instead, let us be driven to a glide, even when we are stuck. Let us have a habit that gets us through the tangled traffic day. **Amen.**

If obstacles are everywhere, cornering us and caging us, let us remove one obstacle at a time. Just one. Let us remove it with vigor and then be glad it is gone. Let us have a ritual of personal congratulation that at least we managed that website or filled out that form or stuck it out through that 800 number which wasn't answering. Let us be those who roll the stones away. **Amen.**

Give me a way to understand that time is not my manager but that I am its manager. Relieve me of the burden of thinking that I can extend my days and help me not waste any more of my days worrying about them. Let me also stop worrying about worrying so much. **Amen.**

When I am afraid that I can't "get it all done," remind me that I never will. Let me rejoice in the great unfinishedness and remember that there is nothing to be frightened of. **Amen.**

Send me a wake-up call about my mortality. Let it ring every day at 6 or 7 or 8 so that when I go to sleep at 10 or 11 or 12 I am aware that I too will pass. **Amen.**

Teach me the Latin words Timor mortis: "fear of death." Permit me the grace not to whine about my mortality by complaining "I don't have enough time." **Amen.**

I have a sense of living in a rented world on borrowed time. Of course I should have feelings about that. How do I pay the rent? The rent is too high. How do I pay the interest on the debt? It is also too high and shames me when I am not paying attention. How do I take what I do have and not mortgage it to a future that may not exist and may not ever have existed? Help me. Then let me help others to help me. Then just let me help others escape the time famine. **Amen.**

I fear that my credit is running out and that I have a bad credit rating, so now everything I borrow is going to cost more. Am I alone? Or is something rigged somewhere? Is it rigged in my spirit or in the system or both? And if it is, how can I be bothered to pray? Doesn't prayer imply trust? And what if I don't trust anything, and no one trusts me to pay my bills? And what if I am out of credit, the cash kind and the human kind? What do I do now? This question is a prayer. **Amen.**

Bring me to terms with the Internet. Help me understand addiction as being wrongly attached to the wrong things and bring me into great attachment to the right things. In this hyper-connected world, I really want to be connected. But I really don't want to be hyper about it. **Amen.**

Remind me that being is passing, nothing more, and nothing less. One second jumps into the other. One week blends into the other. I will wake up one morning and realize I got old when I wasn't looking. Let this surprise delight me not frighten me. **Amen.**

Let my passages be graceful, delicate, aware, tutored. Remind me of my passage from the birth canal into the life canal and now into the death canal, whenever you are ready for me and hopefully I am ready for you, whoever you are, wherever you are. When death comes to me, let me be able to pray my way through it and to it and be ready for it. **Amen.**

If the big philosophers are right and the meaning of our life is to negate our nothingness, then let's start by negating time's grip on our grumpiness. Let us flow through time and let time flow through us and let us never say we are too busy to pray. **Amen.**

Killing time. He said he was just killing time. I wonder what that means. Can prayer be a muse, a wonder, and a pause to think? Yes, it can. **Amen.**

Self-care is not so much wrong as insufficient. These prayers take care of us so we can take care of others. Let us use them as our chief source of renewable energy. Let them be solar and sun, wind and air to us. **Amen.**

Prayer lets the bucket down to our deeper wells and there gathers up the water we need to sustain our thirst for justice. I try here not to make too much or too little out of prayer. I try to show it as a pause that refreshes, a clarity that battles confusion, a peace that passes immediate understanding. Soul strength contrasts to material strength, not replacing it so much as balancing it. Let me not be busy with prayer. **Amen.**

When my time is up, let me be up about my time. Instead of being down about what has evaporated, let me glad about what was. Teach me how to be a historian instead of a futurist. **Amen.**

Teach me the art of the Sabbath, the separation of one time from another. Let me commit civil disobedience, metaphorically by becoming counter-cultural about my time as somebody who keeps a good Sabbath. **Amen.**

When my friend laments to me that she is too busy to see me, let me hear the longing underneath her whining. Let me be a witness to her beyond the whine and let me insist that we can't be too busy for each other. Then let us have a coffee, if not this month, then next month. Let us remember the friendship in the failure to be always present to each other. **Amen.**

Let those who would master us into a state of constant obligation be amused by our refusal to play the game. **Amen.**

From haste and its waste, rescue me, O God. From the time famine and my hunger, deliver me. Slow me down long enough to enjoy my time, here, now. Make me ask the question of where it is I think I am going in such a big hurry. Cure me of the time famine. **Amen.**

I pray for something unpredictable to happen today, like it did yesterday and the day before that. I pray to be so unbusy that I can't possibly predict everything. Give me the gift of seeing my life from a longer view and help me understand how many surprises have already come my way. Then give me the gift of looking forward. Help me become more open to the unpredictable, enjoy greater awareness of underlying causes and meanings, and relax in a largeness of spirit. Let the meetings I go to today and the events I attend tonight be different than I expect them to be, mostly because I behave differently. **Amen.**

Let little things mean a lot today, O God. Coffee breaks, convenient parking spaces, exact change: let each permit me an ounce of joy and gratitude. Let me imagine a day that's less fortunate and improve my perspective about all that has come my way. Keep me so happy about the things I enjoy that I don't have time to worry about what is missing. **Amen.**

Let there be a little razzamatazz today and let it not throw me into a tizzy. Let something unpredicted and unpredictable happen. Let there be a little jazz. A few blues. A little libretto. Solos and choirs. Hear my thanks for the street musician playing in the park or the right Muzak in the elevator or for a great song on the iPod. Or good music on the radio or a walk past a music school while a cellist practices. For Music, music, music. Jazz me up, Holiness, and let music mind my attention. **Amen.**

Let me befriend that word sin. The way we refuse a relationship with God or each other or miss the mark of our full humanity or get curved in on ourselves. Let me pattern myself to a place that is less narrow, less curved in on itself, closer to what is important, like you, O God, our origin and our destination. And from that friendship with sin, let me refuse the narrow space on behalf of the open space, the spacious space. And let me do so with a sense of humor about the narrow spaces as well. **Amen.**

CHAPTER THREE

Prayers to Calm the Monkey's Mind

WE HAD SAILED AT DUSK. We were out for about four hours when our captain turned toward home. Usually, on other sails, she had turned on the engine as we approached the dock. Her boat, a sailing instructor's boat, is docked at the far end of a Miami marina in a corner, a bit of a tight squeeze but not impossible, with the engine going. This night she got a twinkle in her eye, as we turned toward home. "Let's try it without the engine. I think the conditions are right." Minutes later, she added, "We may have to turn the engine on at the last minute so be ready...we won't know till we get close." Moments later we glided, soundlessly and effortlessly and enginelessly, into the berth.

There was a calm in that moment which deserves respect

and attention. It was quieter than I have ever heard. I used to think you couldn't hear quiet. Now I know you can. It was less effort than I have experienced in a long time.

Effort is a persistent intruder in my life: even getting to this sail had required it. I didn't know if I had time, didn't know if it would be enough fun to warrant the time off and away, wondered if I had brought the right dish for my part of the potluck, blah blah blah. I was living in the unpatterned narrow room on the way to the sail at dusk. Like so many internal fusses we have with ourselves, we don't think we have the time to decide what we need to decide, which is surely at least about our engines. By engine I mean the power to pause long enough to know where we want to use what little fuel we have. Internal fusses are not just about how to spend our evenings: they are also about our priorities. They may also be about death, the big kind, not just the turning off of the engine. They may also be about how frittered we want our days and nights to be.

I loved the quiet of the berthing that night. I look forward to the quiet of renewable energies and of energy renewed. I'd like to remember this sail on my deathbed. I want death to be like this for me and for others.

Prayer is a choice to turn the engine off for a while, when conditions are right to glide. It's a way to be powered and empowered without using fossil fuel. Prayer also battles worry, that persistent one about how we don't have time to go sailing or to a potluck supper with friends. Worry is the opposite of calm.

Worry is the uninvited invasion of the present by the past or the future. The past invades with regrets. What if I just hadn't said or done that, or what if she hadn't said that to me or he hadn't done that to me? If those bad things hadn't happened then I could be happy now. Since they did, I can't. We go over the past like a dog gnaws a bone: there is no meat there, but that doesn't keep us from chewing. Often we keep our engines running while chewing.

The most acute kind of worry is when we get down on ourselves for worrying. We not only worry, we worry about how much we worry. "I know I shouldn't worry but I do." We jump into the well of worry and spiral down. Sometimes we even refuse the invitation of friends to sail, so sure are we that we don't have time for fun or calm or renewal.

Here I help you to find an engine-free power, to live on the corner of here-and-now, and to free yourself from foreign occupation. Here I help you to sail as an antidote to worry.

Or think of these prayers like the Boston Tea Party: a revolution by the forces of the present, in the present, overthrowing the wicked spirits with the good ones. We get off the saucer and into the cup of life. I know I am mixing metaphors. Prayer is a renewable energy and loves to mix its metaphors.

When we borrow the power of the spirit to live in the present, we do so trusting that its power is larger than the big stuff we worry about. We imagine ourselves as agents and actors in our lives as opposed to victims. We become the subjects not the objects of our own sentences. We may not be able to control Lyme disease, but we can control our attitude toward it. "We can?" you say. Wondering if Pollyanna is speaking? Pollyanna is actually praying. Prayer not only mixes metaphors, it creates a realm of possibility. Yes, we can. *Si, se puede.*

Permit me to give you the practical reasons not to worry. Worry doesn't help. It wastes time. It blocks positive energy. Like most people, I have plenty of excuses for worrying: I can't remember my passwords. I was on hold with a bank that charged me fifty-nine dollars for an annual fee on a card I don't have. My offspring may have to live through a changed climate, after all that money I spent on braces. My hollyhocks have a disease. The last time I went on that sailing potluck, people didn't like my offering—it was too experimental. (Pineapple upside-down cake with whole wheat flour and wheat germ.) These are perfectly good reasons to worry, and I hope you will join me in legitimating them.

What does it look like to be worry free? We symbolically toss all of the enemy's tea into the spiritual sea. We don't cooperate with our persecutor. We take one rung on the ladder at a time, as our energy permits. We don't give ourselves more to do in any given moment than we can. We do piece work and we do it well. I clean my whole house this way, one corner a day. We also pray, in whatever way is our own. We pause. We turn off one channel and turn on another one. We don't try to be both cup and saucer at the same time. We sail. We glide. We become calm. Every now and then we turn off the engines.

Let me want nothing more than what has been, and let me turn memory into a blessing. Let me be so calm and so tranquil that I sparkle with composure and others are dying to know my secret. Teach us to glide. **Amen.**

We pray, O God, for that thing called integrity, that exciting marriage between our inner and outer lives. Help us to pay attention to our own nourishment and what we put into our bodies, our arms, and our hearts. Help us find energy, to know that health is not so much the absence or disease as it is the presence or vitality. Make us into inner-actives: people who move with grace from the inside out and the outside back again. Help us to be both morally nimble and morally solid. Let us not be afraid of our confusion but rather embrace it with the power of wisdom in you. **Amen.**

Today let us be glittery with gladness, and if not all day, at least this afternoon. **Amen.**

I *carry too much baggage around with me. I am spiritually cluttered. Help me to move beyond the past, beyond revenge. Let me not become the monster I am destroying in my so-called enemy. Let me find the higher revenge and not become like the ones who hurt me.* **Amen.**

T *each me how to refuse to have an enemy at all, including myself. When I find myself obsessing on the darkness, move me into the sunlight and don't let me return to the shade.* **Amen.**

I *didn't do enough for the world yet. I didn't pay attention to your plans for peace and justice. I got lost in my own little world. Now that I am awakened to my mortality, refocus me on your plans. And give me a chance to be part of them. Let me work with the confidence that your time is arriving soon, maybe even tomorrow.* **Amen.**

Everywhere I look I see unfinished work, unfolded laundry, unbuilt additions, unraised children, and unpaid bills. You, who have gotten my attention and stopped me in my tracks, draw near. Show me the difference between the urgent and the important. Show me what really matters and then let me calmly and carefully pursue it. **Amen.**

Let us be eager for the deep water, more afraid of silence than we are of speech, more afraid of risks refused than risks taken. Teach us to be chaos tolerant. And let our witness keep another from drowning. In the name of Spirited People everywhere, who plumb the depths so we can know the way. **Amen.**

When I die, let the work that I've done speak for me. Let the friends I've loved speak for me. Make sure my best suit is laid out for my final days, and let me go out not with a whimper or a whine but with a winsome interest in what, if anything, is next. Let me not waste time on anything but peace and quiet. **Amen.**

Many of us thought we were meant to do something else—write a novel, star in a Broadway play—before the need for health insurance found us. I am not alone in my need to work, at way too many levels. Help me sanctify my work and be less its captive. Let me be calm at my lot in life, even if not satisfied. **Amen.**

Let me not be overwhelmed by my responsibilities today. Let me be grateful for the processes I must go through, at each step along the way. Let my journey lead somewhere, and let me replace anxiety with grace. **Amen.**

Let me repent every minute I have wasted in anxiety and fear. From haste and its waste, rescue me, O God. From the time famine and my hunger, deliver me. Slow me down long enough to enjoy my time, here, now. Make me ask the question of where it is I think I am going in such a big hurry. **Amen.**

Collect our hopes and deliver them from minutiae for minutes and moments of relief and gladness. For time wasted poorly, we confess our sin. For time wasted well, we rejoice. We are so rarely able to just be; we are so often crazed by a destination. Discipline us, Holy Sprits with the calm we see in other holy people. Let us trust the coming of your time, your destination, at your speed. **Amen.**

We are almost always counting. Holy Spirit, teach us, soon, to count our blessings. We are in a terrible hurry. We repent oversleeping and its laziness, insomnia and its anxiety, fogginess and its refusal to focus. We seek vigor and calm and attention. Right us, Holy Spirit. Make us someone you could call friend. **Amen.**

Teach us to pray when we are not burned out but a little fried around the edges. Teach us to stand on the sidewalk and look and listen and pray. Take us to still waters even if skyscrapers surround us. Restore wonder, and let us wonder why we so rarely take the time to wonder. **Amen.**

I pray to learn to love interruptions and not be chained by them. When someone hands me a receipt in the middle of my prayer time, let me be more amused by it than upset. **Amen.**

We pray for compassion, for empathy, and for hearts to stay open to those in worse need than we are. For all those whose lives were ripped away, for all those who have faced rubble with courage. For all those who remain afraid. Grant them and us your peace. **Amen.**

Teach us the meaning of the word repose. Give us peaceful naps. Grant us comfortable chairs and long views outside our windows. Let us enjoy them. **Amen.**

When others bother us with their jumpiness or over-doneness, teach us a method to survive, even to thrive. Let us learn when to walk away, when to cajole, when to challenge, when to break off relationships that just have too much negative energy for us. Teach us how to stick to people, as they and we go through the stalled energy. Let us be people who open up others so that they can open us up as well. **Amen.**

Focus my attention and intention today on what really matters and let me forcefully forget about the rest. **Amen.**

G*ive us a make-under. When we walk, let there be pep in our walk and levity in even our love.*

Most simple zest of all, season me so that I taste good and look good and am not overdone. Zoom my life force into one direction, tasty and tasteful. Let me have time for nothing but calm, so busy am I being seasoned well. **Amen.**

T*each me little tricks to stay calm during my mammogram or colonoscopy. Teach me the art of counting to one hundred slowly or reciting the alphabet backwards. Let me have methods to mind me when I have good reason to be stressed out. Make me a champion deep-breather, and let the rest go by.* **Amen.**

F*or an unfurrowed brow, I pray. Let me become one of those people who can't be bothered with bother. And let me have long chunks of time to attend to the important and not just the urgent.* **Amen.**

The Grand Lady of Downton Abbey *was so rich that she could ask this question, "What is that thing they call a weekend?" What are weekends to us? What are the times we will surely rest? Do we know? And if not, we pray for sufficient calm to find out.* **Amen.**

God *beyond God, you who refuse to worry, help me to change my ways and to pray instead of worry. Don't let me worry if I am praying right. Just let me pray.*

Don't let the future scare me so much. Let me remember that I will not always tend the things I tend today. Let me know that someday others will tend them. Let me tend what I tend the best I can today and let the future tend itself.

Teach us to covet enough difficulty in our lives that we can become fearless or at least less fearful. Remind us how many people find excellence on the route of their troubles overcome. **Amen.**

Replace our uncalmed spirit with a calm one. Give us a sense of the spirit on weekdays. We want to add a sacramental dimension to our lives and we know we can barely spell the word. Still let those of us who don't win spelling contests make holy the way we do the dishes, run the errands that try to run us, manage our intimate lives. Let those sneaky moments of joy become more powerful than those ever present moments of obligation. Let taking care of our daily schedule have sacramentality to it. And if not, let something so big be less of a pain in the neck. **Amen.**

Next time we say the words "real presence," let us say it about something we sensed on a bus ride, a playground, in a gym class. Let Spirit come home and be home to us. **Amen.**

Find us people, O God, who love to hear our old stories and who understand that each time we tell them we are reaching toward your thread in our garment. And give us a way to enjoy the things we have way too many times ourselves. Let us be poised in our own particulars and grace us with a quiet spirit, one that has been quieted by yours. **Amen.**

Let us become people who trust emotions and are good at conflict. Let us be people who don't dread the morning so much as welcome it for its new opportunities, mysteries, and problems. When we say the word challenge, let it not be ironic. Lead us to praise for what is and release us from lament for what isn't. **Amen.**

Give us a giggle every now and then at how seriously we take it all, and let us learn to enjoy the whole megillah, made whole in our very appreciation of it. **Amen.**

CHAPTER FOUR

Prayers for the Great Recession to Recede

A FATHER TELLS THE STORY OF HIS son at Thanksgiving. It was the first year that the family was gathering at the son's house instead of the father's. The son's grandmother and father's mother was the senior at the table. Someone said that stuffing should no longer be put in the turkey because it was potentially unhealthy. The grandmother went off. She sputtered and spewed and took the opportunity to let everyone know that she was not just tired of new ideas, she was just plain tired. The conversation deteriorated. People left the table with spiritual indigestion.

Later in the afternoon, the son came to the father, put his hands on his father's shoulders, and said, "Dad, it is not your fault."

When it comes to the great stagnation of this early part of the twenty-first century, the first and only prayer is here. It is not our fault. We can't say that to ourselves or to each other enough. We really can't. Taking responsibility for something larger than ourselves is a marvelous form of grandiosity. Prayer helps us get to our right size.

Sometimes we find ourselves saying, "My get-up-and-go has got-up-and-went." We may even have heard our own grandparents say that. We understand fatigue. The longer we live, the more we understand it. Many of us are tired of this first decade of the twenty-first century. It has brought us terrorist attacks, mass murders of children in Connecticut, Hurricane Sandy and its weather sisters and brothers, plus one story of economic decline after another. We call it recession, but we could also call it recession fatigue. It sometimes appears the whole country—along with the church—has moved into a narrative of decline and is grumpily living in that story.

Many say, "I am so tired of being tired." Still others declare that there is no vacation time long enough to recover an imagined previous energy. The story of decline has long arms and reaches into many corners of our lives. Energy depletes and we search for a way to recession proof our souls, so that they may be strong in changing the narrative of decline. Many tell me that they are not just empty nest but empty of a sense of the next.

How can we frame the question of energy in such a way as to be gentle to our fatigue—while also combating it? How can we be kind to the grandmother who has just enough the proper way to cook a turkey? As well as to the others at her table? Can we be both tired and renewable, even long after we don't believe in our own renewal? Can we find ways to say something other than decline? It doesn't have to be replaced with that overdone optimism of the progressive. But it can be replaced with something like calm and its refusal to live in a sullied present as though it were the future as well.

Prayer changes the stories we tell ourselves. Unlike morning and evening prayers, this kind of prayer is a little more of the midday kind. This kind of prayer has its boots on the ground. When others tell us how bad things are—and how they plan to get worse—we reverse field. When older people tell us they are tired of younger ideas, we comfort the conversation. We say something hopeful or positive. Not grandly so, but instead quietly so. We place our hands on each other's shoulders. Or we say something like an absolution: it is not your fault.

Pete Seeger, who died in the time I was writing this, said that the key to the future is finding the good stories and helping each other tell them. Prayer agrees.

Prayer that recession-proofs the soul may be as simple as saying, "Yes, I hear you." It must be awful living with long-term unemployment or being a college grad and unable to get a job or having to live at home when you are thirty. I know you worry about your retirement. Or I know you know how to stuff a turkey. I know you worry about the big economy and the big government moving into your small life. But come with me to the quiet corner and imagine another way. Let me assure you that everything is going to be all right, even though I don't know how yet. Prayer is not as big an item as people imagine it to be. Prayer is more like a pause than anything else. It is that blessed reflection that follows excessive action, even a lifetime of excessive action. Workaholics understand better than others what it means to be tired—and to not know how to quit. We do think we are our jobs—and we are not. We are what we do plus what we don't do.

Prayer doesn't offer solutions to the great stagnation so much as it questions it. Prayer changes fields. It is a conversation in which the power of something larger than the political economy of the present appears. When we encourage our friends, we are actually encouraging ourselves. Prayer is not so much a "Yes, but" as it is a "Yes, and." I would never suggest correcting the person who wants to tell you another story of a decline. By all means, agree with him or her. Recognize the suffering. Acknowledge the suffering. "I hear you" is an important thing to say, especially if you really mean it. Then, after hearing, we can create an assurance by touch or by words or by smile that things are not always going to be this way and that they are going to be OK. Confess that you don't know how. You will find yourself in a form of prayer. You will be naming a hope. You will be dragging yourself and your associate out of a well, the kind that is so deep there are no longer ladders down there. You will learn that "it" is not your fault, even though you have response-ability.

H*elp us to get over our sense that the party is over. Help us to start a new party, O God. Let us feast as often as possible and every now and then let it not cost a lot of time or money.* **Amen.**

I *am tired of hearing the word* recession *and so are most of the people I know. Long after this great stagnation is gone, there will still be people outside, people left behind, people without enough. In this moment we live now with an uninvited less. Many have lived in our new home for a long time. We are pawns in someone else's game. I pray today for enough calm for what is gone so that I can face its loss. I pray for time to think through the clouds to the possible silver linings. I pray to not get scared, for others or myself. I pray for a generosity of spirit that does not recede.* **Amen.**

Our hands shake and we feel the rush of adrenaline in our veins. We don't know when the shaking will stop or when it will start up again. We are not ready to deal with icebergs melting or seas rising. We know these things are not our fault but are still our responsibility. Give us spiritual adrenaline so we can imagine a world of clean air for our grandchildren. **Amen.**

Some say that the only way to get into heaven is to have a letter of recommendation from the poor. That strikes me as a lousy self-serving reason to care for the poor! Get me better reasons, O God, and before it is all over, make sure my life mattered to someone else. When I fear for my future, forbid me saying "Others are worse off than me." Connect me with sincerity to my poverty and that of others. **Amen.**

When I find myself saying that I am less badly off than others, dust off that idea in my brain and in my speech. Let me ask why I am defending my sense of poverty by excusing it. Let me confront my own poverty without comparing it to others. And let me be a force for wealth for myself and those I don't even know but just imagine are "worse off" than me. Confront our collective insecurity as often as possible. **Amen.**

Teach us to attend to the poor and the failed as much as we bother with the rich and successful. Let us say something nice to somebody who we think doesn't need any help. For those who have stopped looking for a job and struggle not to hear others call them lazy, for those whose unemployment check has run out, for those who used to think they were going somewhere and now know they are not, for all displaced by the great stagnation, we pray. If we are one of them, we especially pray for ourselves. And if not, let us at least have compassion for those we imagine as "lazy." Let us not blame people for poverty but instead shoulder the weight of making a new economy for all. **Amen.**

W*e ask for courage, for patience, for trust, for the refusal to substitute addictive calms for the real thing. We ask for permission to see ourselves in each person, to relate and touch. Dream in us a dream for a secure world for all of us.* **Amen.**

P*revent me from becoming a make-believe Marxist, thinking that the economy is everything and that I am nothing. Prevent me from overdoing the material and help me overdo something spiritual, even if it is just getting control of my attitude. Every day has an adventure, deep within its cells. Some are early cancer; others are cancer's tamers. Some moments contain opportunities that only come once and can lead to joy; others are just plain mistakes, mistakes we seem to have to make. Teach me the difference, O God, someday soon. And teach us what we mean by a growing economy.* **Amen.**

Whenever we see a corner, or are cornered, or hope we have turned a corner, make not fun of our hopes for a future. Instead, humor us and, if you are sick of that, understand us. We thank you in advance. **Amen.**

Why are some others and I so lucky? Grace me with an explanation or two, Blessed One. Point me in luck's deeper direction, that road called gratitude. **Amen.**

Even when blessed, I fear the loss of blessing. Will you keep my secret with me? I promise not to "out" anyone, and I also promise not to live my life in an insecure closet. Help me. Let my outside appearance match my inner life. **Amen.**

My heart has two enemies: the fullness of the empty and the emptiness of the full. I do enjoy contradictions, but this one is getting me down. How can I be so rich and so poor at the same time? And what do I do about those who don't have the choice to complain but must simply carry on? Help me with my enemies and help me get past my enemies to my friends. **Amen.**

Let me find something grand and worthy and put my name on it, like a pipe organ or an endowment of light paperbacks to a heavy library or a garden of daffodils or a stone labyrinth. Let me last somehow. **Amen.**

O God, let me not eat a tomato without knowing its source or its sacredness. Let me never treat any human being as an object either. In your name and the name of the outsiders. **Amen.**

Help me understand the paradox and privilege of progressivism, the way we go to summer camps, travel overseas, and still hope for a larger world for people who have never left home. **Amen.**

If a check comes from the restaurant tonight, O God, let me pray that the farmer and the waiter will eat as well as I have. Make sure I answer no when asked, "Are you still working on that?" I was never working on it. And barring a granting of these hopes, help me to understand the meaning of the word "tip." **Amen.**

We long to be a people of radical contentment, a people linked to each other by joy, at home with each other in peace, alive to each other in hope and friends of the great grounding earth. Plant our feet firmly on high ground and let us not waver. **Amen.**

We wonder, O God, if it was your intention to scare us with tsunamis, hurricanes, earthquakes, and floods. Is it plague time? How much dare I worry about mortgage rates and still be human? How can we protect the calm that we need thrice as much under such circumstances? Will you be our source and our guide? **Amen.**

In a world where clutter has consultants and storage is a growth industry, relieve us of our stuff. Let us be a people who are free of it, no matter how much we have of it. Let our closets be places of memories, not oppressions. May our cellars be foundations of friendships, not worries. Teach us the calm of having things without letting things have us. **Amen.**

Let me find a way to be "out" and not hidden, transparent but not foolish, open but not stupid. Let me find a way to live by a deeper set of laws than those of getting ahead and protecting myself. Limit my exposure to the small stuff and increase my exposure to that which is large. **Amen.**

When this day gets out of control as so many do, with anxiety about money tipping me into anxiety about just about everything, remind me of where I was going when I started and where I intended to be when I finished. Reset my map and let me start over and over again, in the right direction. I know how to be lost. Help me be found. **Amen.**

When the day is done and I am undone, O God, restore me. Let me try again to do what I'm meant to do. And if I'm not meant for anything in particular, orient me toward a doing and a being that is useful. Let me be part of the free market, of love, affection, respect, usefulness, whether I get paid well for it or not. **Amen.**

Let little things mean a lot today, O God. Coffee breaks, subway tokens, the parking space near the train: let each permit me an ounce of joy and gratitude. Let me imagine a day of less good fortune and improve my point of view on what has come my way. **Amen.**

When I die, let the work that I've done speak for me. Let the friends I've loved speak for me. Make sure my best dress is laid out for my final days, and let me go out not with a whimper or a whine but with a winsome interest in what, if anything, is next. Give me a sense of progress toward my grave. **Amen.**

When we sit down to eat, let us give thanks from our hearts, praying that the day comes soon when everyone will eat as well as we will, today and tomorrow. **Amen.**

May we start every meal giving thanks for what we have. May we miss strawberries less in winter and learn to live with less oil and more thanksgiving. Turn our middle aging into less of a muddle. Turn me from someone who won't be good at growing old into someone who will excel at it. Let the price of my pension be appropriately important, and no more, and allow my whole life's legacy to gain in my view. Let my habits be those of a person who wants to look good, feel good, and live long. Along the way, amuse me and let me be amusing. **Amen.**

Jesus said, "Take the log out of your own eye." It confuses me. Am I ready for the adventure of introspection? Am I ready to see without blinders? I pray yes, but I think not. Open me up, O God, the way I would like others to be open. Let my worth be more than what is in my bank account. **Amen.**

We live in interesting times, where we overuse the word problem. *Cure us of the problem of our hometown, the problem of gentrification; the problem of global warming, the problem of problems, and the way they make us look back. Free us for a future, one not free of problems but also not dominated by them.* **Amen.**

Help us open the doors that we think are closed.

Help us do more and more with less and less.

Economize us, O God—not to be cheap, but to find feast in the small.

Let a new perspective enlighten our days.

For a little peace, a little purpose, and a lot of satisfaction, we pray. Let us go to the marketplace with joy and hope. Guarantee that we rise with vigor and retire with grace, and not just today but in an alpha and omega way. **Amen.**

Ritualize our days so that time is ours and not outsourced. Cure us of the time famine and let flow from start to finish be ours. Keep us from being jumpy and bopping from one thing to the next. Grant us the gift of focus, the freedom to work on one obstacle at a time. **Amen.**

Let us find the sacred deep within the ordinary, in the sweetness in our coffee and the bread on our table. Let us never miss a chance to praise what is good—and let the rest go by. **Amen.**

When we eat on the run let us not forget to say thanks even for our haste and the plastic and Styrofoam, which is its container. And keep our eye on the prize of a tablecloth in our near future. **Amen.**

I *pray, O God, for that thing called integrity, and an exciting marriage between inner and outer life. Help me pay attention to my own nourishment. Help me find energy, to know that health is not so much the absence of disease as the presence of vitality. When I fear a fundamental loss of tone, engage me in the practice of health and well-being. Universalize an assurance of health, whether I have health "insurance" or not.* **Amen.**

G*ood and Gracious God, we pray for a deepening of our hospitality. Let us turn from the words of hostility to the words of hospitality. Teach us compassion for all those standing with us in the soup line, job line, emergency room. We are neither their enemy, nor they ours. Help us to understand that.* **Amen.**

I*f the recession and the stagnation have not come our way, let us master the mystery of why. Let us be open to our luck without bragging about it. Let us find a way to share our wealth.* **Amen.**

CHAPTER FIVE

Road-Strengthening Prayers for the Commuting Soul

MOST OF US ARE IN MOTION MOST of our days. We commute to work or walk to work or bike to work. We take the 8:31 or the 6:36. We pack our lunch or forget to pack our lunch. I call my own days in New York City "uptown, downtown, all around the town." Mercifully, I now have a senior pass for the subway and thus pay a lot less than $2.50 a ride, plus transfers. My work involves four or five subways plus buses a day. Each is an adventure, unless they turn into a time sink because the A train isn't running or the M3 is involved with a "situation," which usually means that the bus driver can't extricate the wheelchair and we are waiting for assistance. Or that someone at Fifty-Ninth Street had a heartattack. Or that someone uptown stole a purse. Commuting in New

York—and many other places—is a crapshoot. Traffic may or may not intervene with our progress.

One of my congregants commutes on a scooter to her physical therapy and doctor's appointments. She is only forty-four. She has stiff person syndrome and can't walk, has lost her job, and is on disability. She has to beg the bus drivers to strap her in. Many say they just can't. They don't have time. They will get off schedule. She often has to ask others to hold her chair so she won't fall out of it again. The bus drivers are professional commuters, right? Always rushing to stay on time. Always worrying that they could lose their own job. My favorite New Yorkers are the ones who say thank you to the driver as they get off the bus. They are praying.

We often call commuting hell. Learning to pray in motion can change that. This kind of prayer is not just an efficiency move—although this entire book is kind of like the Henry Ford version of prayer. By that I mean, it is a way to steal back time to pray from lost time. It is a way to become tricky about prayer, sneaky about prayer, finding the holy in the ordinary. It is piecework on life's assembly line.

Many theologians tell us that we have been wrong in our division of the sacred and the profane. You know that dualism: going to church services is sacred and driving your car is profane. Sunday is Sabbath; Monday is for all the bad things you want to do or have to do. Instead, we now understand (or hope) that the real division is between the sacred and the desecrated. Monday can be as holy as Sunday. Work as holy as worship. Travel as holy as staying put. Out as holy as in, and in as holy as out. Outward as holy as inward, and inward as holy as outward.

In that frame, desecrating commuting, as though it was not time or not living, is a spiritual mistake. Plus, when you tell yourself you don't have time to pray, there is the commute sitting there with its robes on, asking you to participate in a sacred kind of time.

Many people have already figured this out and enjoy their commute. They read on the train. They listen to music in the car. They install Bluetooth and talk to their parents or children while driving. The Long Island Railroad used to offer classes in one of its car. Amtrak used to have a piano car on the Montrealer. Commuting time becomes almost sacred when we do something with it—including its perpetual delays—and it is desecrated when we let the motion alone be our master.

Prayer on the road can be something like this. Review your whole life and give thanks for the good stuff and ask for forgiveness for the not so good. This kind of review can really eat up the miles, especially if you have lived a while. Or pick a year and enjoy trying to remember it. What might you have done differently? What proved consequential? What did not prove consequential? Who cares? Do you? Are there amends to be made?

Or review your last few vacations and enjoy them again. Or plan a different kind of birthday for your partner or your son. What is the funniest gift you could give? In other words, introspection is a form of prayer. Why not rejoice when the time to think shows up at your seat on the bus?

If you listen to the news, pray for peace or for the last terrible story you heard and the people who were affected by it. If you listen to music, let it carry you to some place that is composed. You might even listen to hymns or reggae and find the God they are describing.

Often we are alone on the road. Solo commuting is crazy and also has its quiet wonders. Commuting is a great time to get to know ourselves. If life reviews bore you, do life exploration instead. Imagine yourself five years from now, or ten. Take pictures of your future and then plan and head there. Aim for something. Aiming is also a form of prayer.

Prayer while commuting is not just a form of efficiency— although it is surely that. It removes the greatest excuse of all: that we don't have time to pray. It restores a sense of self-respect, that we are indeed in charge of our time and that the highway is not. Prayer while commuting is efficiency plus fun. It re-sacralizes what has been desecrated, and way too often what has been desecrated is our sense of owning our own time. Own your own time on the road and you will find a great rush of spiritual relaxation, what some call peace.

When stuck in the middle seat on the plane, let me find a way to dive far enough inside that I forget that I am leaning on someone I don't even know. **Amen.**

When drinking yet another cup of coffee out of another Styrofoam cup, let me enjoy it and not become too high and mighty about how I ought to be sitting at a table with a ceramic cup and saucer. Let me come to terms with the way things are now, not be too nostalgic about a then that never was, and never give up hoping that the world of the coffee break will return. **Amen.**

When eating out, let me not forget to give thanks. Let me not forget to eat slowly. And to digest my food. And to overtip. And to remember the dishwasher. **Amen.**

Teach me the difference between being cheap and being frugal. Let me find a frugal way to ignore the miles on the way home today by amusing myself with a subject larger than the road signs. Let me thank everybody I've already met and everybody I will meet. Let me find a way to be gratefully on time, even when it is slowing me down on my way home. **Amen.**

When I am late for pick-up at the day care, and even then I manage to feel exasperated about my day rather than grateful for the women who are caring for my children, take me out of the world where a cloak of harmony covers up the real tensions of bearing and raising children, into a world where gender wars cease and mothers have all they need to feed their children. Take me from a small to an enlarged place. And tomorrow let me be on time. **Amen.**

Let every red light become a signal to pray. And let me not care if someone honks at me for slowing them down on the way to their heart attack. Let me be glad I'm not going where they are going. **Amen.**

Let us be people who cross borders and allow borders to cross us. Let me know I am in a place when I am in a place, even if I have been stuck all day in a windowless hotel meeting room or a cubby in a large office building. When I am in Chicago, let me know I am in Chicago. When I am in the same office I go to every day, let me know I am in that office that has an address and a zip code. When we travel, help us to long to get home. When we are home, let us long to travel. Mix us up in such a beautiful way that we never send one of those post cards, "having a great time, wish I was here." And always let us know other people are in other time zones, being human too. **Amen.**

Let me notice what is clear on the highway: there is horizon, there is space, there is dawn or dusk or somewhere in between. Let me appreciate that which is not manicured or overdesigned. Let me notice what I drive through, whether it is a great prairie or a great swamp or a place in between me and my people, me and my home. Let my travels broaden me. **Amen.**

Open up the doors of heaven in an unlikely place and let the dawn or the dusk surprise me with a new version of color. Let entrance ramps carry meaning for me, even as the ubiquitous waffles in every highway motel cause me to be curious. How did they get so popular? How can I be a part of the great traffic jam that my commute is? **Amen.**

M*ake me see someone new today at that train station, someone I have never seen before: the custodian or the guy with the coffee. Let me be a person who understands that spirituality is a connectedness in the most unlikely of places. Let me not obscure those who work but attend to them.* **Amen.**

L*et me understand the meaning of* adult *as someone who goes places and does things and is not bruised by it. Let there be choice in the way I move from place to place, and if there isn't, help me to go home.* **Amen.**

W*hen I worry about the food I eat on the road, remind me of the best cookbooks, those who imagine a way to eat a quick breakfast. Let me learn to love Tupperware and to carry my food with me so that I am always eating what I want, not "just what I can find."* **Amen.**

Let there be a chant to my commute: a song I sing, a hum I hum, something that connects me to the deep rhythm of ancient song. **Amen.**

Let me not be a secessionist gambling with civilization but a participant. Let me commute to community and be a part of solutions and back ways to get there. Let me truly have a global positioning system. **Amen.**

There is a reign of error in so many parts of our lives. We probably shouldn't be driving, single file in single occupancy cars. How can we find more human ways to commute? Let us meditate on one utopia after another. **Amen.**

In a world where everyone is looking for their hyphen, their particular mixture, let me see what is hidden. Am I a corporate executive or something smaller? Am I a working mother or something larger? Who am I when people ask me who I am? What really ought to be on my nametag during the meeting? **Amen.**

Let me not be overwhelmed by my commute today, but instead let me enjoy the journey. While the notion of life as a journey is an apt metaphor, when the journey becomes the dominant reality, it begins to lose its appeal. Let my journey lead somewhere and let me find grace in place of fear. Let me live beyond ground travel and its arrangements into something like flow. **Amen.**

There is a fatigue on the road that sometimes can't be described. Like children, we just don't know if we are ever going to get there. Our hearts are scabbed, our knees have lost their cartilage, we're not sure we can take much more, and yet we know more may come. Give us enough healing to go on—and encourage us in small simple ways. **Amen.**

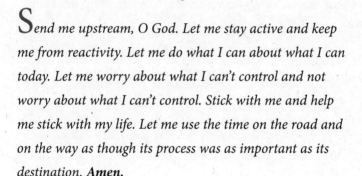

Send me upstream, O God. Let me stay active and keep me from reactivity. Let me do what I can about what I can today. Let me worry about what I can't control and not worry about what I can't control. Stick with me and help me stick with my life. Let me use the time on the road and on the way as though its process was as important as its destination. **Amen.**

May the road rise up to greet us and may we rise up to greet the road. **Amen.**

Thank you for my radio and my CDs and my music along the way. Thank you for a good talk show and intelligent people who bother to call in. Thank you for music that soothes or excites or amazes. And don't tell anybody how badly I sing when I sing along. **Amen.**

When we realize we are in tatters and need a good, solid breakdown, give us, O God, permission to crumble. Then send an old song or a funny memory. Let it have an unoccupied brainwave. Grant us the peace of a long sit in a chair or a really good sigh. When we are able to rise again, let renewal show us what to do or be or say next. Grant us the peace of knowing the tatters will return, and so will the rising. Make it clear to us that we can't do or be or say everything. **Amen.**

CHAPTER SIX

Prayers for the Broken Heart

WHEN LOVE GOES WRONG, it goes wrong in a viral way. Even ice cream doesn't taste as good any more. When love goes right, it also goes viral—even stale bread tastes good. We use the word *viral* a lot these days and love the power of the swift and the way viral means a lot of attention is going in the same direction. Viral used to be negative, as in we have a virus. Viral can still be negative or positive. When love goes right, there is a viral plus. When love goes wrong, there is a viral minus.

I can show you best what I mean by viral by exploring the invasive species, the purple loosestrife. The purple loosestrife is a marsh plant. It actually looks beautiful in bloom. It is purply pink. It can be eight feet tall. You have seen them everywhere because they have all but taken over marshes in New York, New Jersey, and Minnesota. Maryland long ago called out the plant militia.

The plant goes rapidly into a monoculture, knocking everybody else out: cattails and rush, even salt hay. It also changes the way water flows and destroys the food sources for many marsh animals, especially turtles. It came to this country in the nineteenth century on sailing ships and grew by attaching its pointy seeds to people's clothing and letting them pay the fare to take the seeds elsewhere. It can have over a thousand seeds per plant. The loosestrife can loose strife in a wide area. It also knows how to grow by roots as well as seeding. Like love, even a little love for a short time, it is very beautiful in bloom. You know its difficulty when you see that it takes over all the space for anything else.

There is an antidote to it, and the antidote is a beetle. The Galerucella beetle, which is even smaller than a loosestrife seed, can and does stop it. It is a simple small solution to a large invasive problem. When we lose love for whatever reason—whether ditched or divorced or discovered that it is true that our parents don't really like us—we have to watch the viral. We have to make sure that lost love doesn't take over the whole state.

Prayer is a lot like that beetle. It stops the negative energy in such a way as to make room for the positive energy. You can find the renewable energy of Spirit in contrast to the loosing of strife. These are the questions for those whom love has disappointed. They are also the questions for those whom love has cheered. When you are gone from this planet, will there be more of a monoculture or more biodiversity? Did you renew or deplete? Did you find a way to love after you were unloved?

Forget the big stuff for a while and think about your office or your home. Will you have crowded out native plants or learned to live among them? Will there be more turtles, more slow things, or fewer? Will you have changed the way water flows and, if so, will the flow help or hurt other animals and plants? Will you have increased the food sources available to people? In other words, will you be so Spirited that you can coexist happily, or will you be so demonic that you will have to wipe out others to survive? Better yet, will love harm you virally and permanently, or will love lost bring you to a deeper you, one with better goals than to be loved?

If you don't want the fully renewable resource of the Spirit, then you could just become a Galerucella beetle and stop the bad spirits from invading. But why let the beetles have all the fun? Instead, we can learn the forces of positive invasion and renewable energy.

Prayer is the practice of positive invasion, loosing the peaceful virals into the world and its system. Nobody can stop you from praying, even those who didn't love you right or well or long enough.

I love Psalm 139:14 which says, "I am fearfully and wonderfully made." Just saying that psalm sometimes tells me that I am going to be surprised—not confirmed—by what will come next. Prayer renews a capacity to sparkle with composure, even after rejection. Prayer can turn the direction of the viral around, even if we were jilted or under-parented, cheated on or cheated. We are fearfully and wonderfully made. We are so fearfully and wonderfully made that we can change the environment, one beetled bite at a time.

I *can't go on another online dating service. I just can't do it. There is no one for me out there, and now there is no longer any me left in here. Help me.* **Amen.**

My husband and I know we have been done wrong. We want yesterday back, and it won't come. Steady us, O God, steady us. I used to love him and I no longer do. What can I do next to renew my marriage? **Amen.**

Forgive me for not trying harder at the right time. Forgive me for trying too hard. Forgive me for my loneliness and let me reach out with just one more try today. **Amen.**

Create in me a capacity for loneliness. Teach me to be alone and well and full. Let me also remain so curious that others will be curious about me. **Amen.**

Slow me down, O God. Slow me down enough to see the opportunities for relationship all around me. Let me stop trying so hard. Let me not race to full or relax in empty, but let me pace myself so that I know the difference between too much and too little, between fish to eat and fish to nurture me spiritually. Clarify us. Deepen us. And grant us your peace. **Amen.**

Let me bet my romantic life on the spirit in this day. Let me be alert to assets outside me as well as assets inside me. Let it put a wiggle in my walk and a giggle in my talk. **Amen.**

Remove from me the deep pessimism of this loss. Remind me that when one window shuts, another opens. **Amen.**

Help me tell her that I don't want to talk about her loss any more. That I want her to get on with it. That I am tired of her repetitions. Help me find a way to help her see a new day on the horizon. **Amen.**

May we find serenity amid the chaos, grace under pressure, and romance in the ordinary. **Amen.**

Truly romantic people and truly erotic people are always in love with something and always in trouble with somebody. Let me risk romance and Eros, again and again. **Amen.**

Most pungent zest of all, season me so that I taste good and look good and am good. Zoom my life force in one direction, tasty and tasteful. **Amen.**

I tried as hard as I could and I failed. I got divorced because I couldn't mate in captivity any longer. Forgive me and let me forgive myself and my partner. **Amen.**

Grace what is left of me now that she is gone. Let me do what she would want me to do, which is to move forward. We said, "Till death do us part." Now we are parted. Let us move on, slowly, carefully, with tenderness toward what was and hope in what can yet be. Let her memory empower me. **Amen.**

Teach me to pray, even when I can't or won't. Teach me to pause and think, resolve and trust. Let my prayers for success in love be said, not with cynicism or with irony but with a foot in front of me, walking toward the future. **Amen.**

For sex and romance, hands and feet, neurons and veins, manicures and pedicures, massages and a great longing to be touched deeply, for our daily bread and digestion.

Let the last words on my lips at the end of every day and at the end of my life be "Thanks be to God." No matter the betrayal, after the divorce, before the next date, let me be someone who is alright alone as well as happily together. Let me be a both/and kind of person. **Amen.**

When I look in the mirror, permit me to be happy at what I see. Take criticism away. Let the double chin amuse me. Let me be glad to have the looks and look I have and not long for love too much. Let me not sell myself or improve myself for someone, but instead let me find someone who loves me the way I am. **Amen.**

When I look at my lover, permit me to be happy at what I see. Take criticism away. Let their flaws amuse me. Let me love him or her just the way they are. **Amen.**

Remove performance from romance so that romance may thrive. **Amen.**

Let someone send me a flower today. Even if it is only one. Let me send someone flowers today, a large and expensive bunch. **Amen.**

When all I can think about is how love has wronged me, fill me with love for someone else who is like me. Let me be the golden-rule girl and take it from there. **Amen.**

Let me touch my wedding ring with love, review the wedding album with love, or at least dust the picture in the picture frame on the mantel. Let me remember the promises I made and give me the capacity to keep them. **Amen.**

When love fails me, drive me down deep to find out if I have failed to love. Then bring me back to another try, even if it means another failure. **Amen.**

Love doesn't fail everybody. Let me refuse to generalize no matter how hurt I am. Send me to the park where I can watch the elderly couples holding hands or the daughter taking the mom out to feed the birds or the boy escorting his aunt to the ice cream truck. Remind me that love succeeds as often as it fails—and send me to the park with some birdseed in my hand, money for ice cream in my pockets, and two hands that are ready to hold. **Amen.**

When all is said and done, let my effect on the world be flowing water, many cultures, many ways, much diversity of plant and animal. Let me be one of the people who found the secret of going on after we have been hurt. Let Darwin's evolution be revealed in me. Let me more than survive. Let me make something really beautiful. **Amen.**

When love fails me or I fail love, remind me of those three often repeated sentences from the Lord's Prayer: *forgive us our debts as we forgive our debtors. Or forgive us as our sins as we forgive those who sin against us. Or forgive us our trespasses as we forgive those who trespass against us.* **Amen.**

From the Lord's Prayer:

Our Father which art in heaven, hallowed be thy name. Thy kingdom come. Thy will be done in earth, as it is in heaven. Give us this day our daily bread. And forgive us our debts, as we forgive our debtors. And lead us not into temptation, but deliver us from evil: for thine is the kingdom, and the power, and the glory, forever. **Amen.** (Matthew 6:9-13 KJV)

CHAPTER SEVEN

When Hurt, Ill, or Lost

I HAVE MISPLACED MY MAGIC WAND. I can't help the forty-four-year-old brilliant school teacher get over the sudden onslaught of stiff person's syndrome. I can't help the sixty-five-year-old woman who has a terminal cancer, one that will close her throat soon, causing her to choke to death. I can't stop the twenty-six-year-old from taking crystal meth even though his parents are desperately assuring me that I can. I lost my magic wand. Truthfully, I never had one. I just sometimes make that sick joke to exit a chemotherapy ward.

Many people are afraid that their sickness of mind or body is their own fault. Maybe it is. Or at least it is to the extent that we don't use all the medicines available to us. By this default, we do participate in our own suffering. Prayer can assuage suffering, if not fix it. Wellness is possible even when we are sick. Jesus was right when he said, "Your faith has made you well."

My three-year-old grandson got stuck under the ottoman. He should never have been climbing under there in the first place. It had loose springs and lots of dust bunnies. He had been warned. When his parents pulled him out, terrified, because he really was stuck mid-tomb, they brilliantly parented him. "What do you want to say to the ottoman?" First, he told the ottoman to get out of the house and never come back. Then he told it that it could stay if it would behave and never trap him again. He also said he wouldn't climb under it any more. Well-digested personal aims join human family and community. They keep us from slowly hurting ourselves by hiding under masters unworthy of our humanity. They help us be well, even when we are sick. They challenge sickness by naming many forms of health. One is not participating in our own trouble.

Spiritual mastery through well-digested personal aim gives us a way out of the tomb so many of us crawl into while living. When we get sick, especially if we haven't learned to take care of ourselves spiritually, we often lose our aim. We think there is nothing left of us when there might be.

Aiming to pray is something anybody, anywhere, under any circumstance can do. There are no ottomans in our way. Just waking up to prayer, in something as simple as saying "Thank you God for October 1," which is when I am writing this, or going to sleep naming those you love and floating your love of them into the universe can help "viral" a culture of time feast instead of time famine. When we ritualize our days, we become stronger against the ottomans. When we ritualize our days before we get sick, we have an ally when we do get sick.

Of course, you can just stay under the ottoman and beg somebody to help you get out. Or you can blame someone for what you are not and what you don't have. Blame is always a great cul-de-sac while sick. If we can just find out whose fault it is, maybe we will feel better. Usually that blaming makes us feel worse instead. Why does blame make us feel worse? Because it is a big excuse not to pray or to know the peace that passes understanding. It is to obey orders that really aren't that authentic or strong anyway. It is to accuse instead of accept. Once that habit begins, it is hard to break it.

A better habit is to learn the art of mystery as an explanation. Mystery explains the awful things that happen to us as well as appreciating life's grandeur. Once I was in Hawaii for a week, and I made a game out of counting the many rainbows that came each day. One day I saw fourteen! I said to my daughter late that afternoon, "Is it wrong to want to see one more today?" She said absolutely, and she was right. There is no point in greed. Mystery manages to enjoy fourteen rainbows and to remember, while sick in bed, that happy mysteries occur as well as horrible ones.

The two sentences I have enjoyed the most since cancer became the shark in my formerly serene swimming pool: "I have lived so long and so well and had such a good life. How could I possibly ask for more?" There is a gratitude in looking back that is not possible for the cancer survivor looking forward. Looking forward, we get greedy. Looking back, we develop gratitude. The gratitude lets what days we have be full and good.

We can get in our own way by wanting more rainbows than a Hawaii afternoon can offer. And, by the grace of God, we can get out of our own way. Indeed, we can move from greed to grace by braving our own excess. How? By wanting less, not more, and learning to love what we have.

Count the rainbows you see every day. Make a life list. Don't ask for more. Ok, maybe just one more. If we manage sickness with a sense of mystery, prayers of gratitude as well as grief become possible for us.

When my body hurts, let me still love it. Let what I know of life not be invaded by illness, and if it is, remind me that wellness is one thing and cure is another. **Amen.**

Hhelp me to find a shawl or a blanket that I imagine is a good friend. Let me wear it when cold, let it warm me, and let me not be afraid. **Amen.**

Let what is wine in me not turn to vinegar. Let what is left of bread in me not mold. Let there be something left at the end of the day. Let that be my healing. **Amen.**

Energy and Spirit, please amuse us today so that we may amuse others. Let us laugh, or at least giggle. Let us not relinquish all time to sickness but only the part it must take. **Amen.**

Focus my attention and intention today on what really matters, and let me forcefully forget about the rest. Make sure I thank someone. Let me smile at the nurse or doctor. Let me understand that I am one of many to them, even though they are so much more to me. **Amen.**

Let me imagine something I've always wanted to do today and let me do it: peruse old albums; organize a drawer or a shoebox; watch an old video or movie; listen to organ music on the radio. Let me steal back a part of my life from illness. Let me make a habit of doing that, even if just for fifteen minutes a day. **Amen.**

When you pass through the waters, I will be with you; and through the rivers, they shall not overwhelm you" (Isaiah 43:1). When death knocks on my door, let me not fear it. Let me remember the waters of the birth canal that brought me here and the great Jordan of our imagination and how it will take me home. ***Amen.***

Your faith has made you well," said Jesus. But what if I don't have any faith? Hear me cry, hear me groan, and don't make fun of me. Very little really makes sense to me. I need someone to understand that. Is it you? ***Amen.***

Help me understand if I want touch or don't want touch, and help me learn how to tell other people, who are as confused as I, about what I want. ***Amen.***

*W*here there is stress, manage it.
Where there is fear, chase it.
Where there is control, tame it.
Where there is diffidence, dare it to be bold.
Let there be no outsiders here. Not one.
Including me. **Amen.**

*W*e are sometimes so sick and tired of being sick and
*tired that we forget to give. Gifts mount in us, but all we
can manage is a nod. Remove us from the place called
sick-and-tired into the place called well-and-motivated. At
least for an hour a day.* **Amen.**

*T*he chaplain in the oncology ward said that the best
*prayer was "to meet with dignity and grace whatever
comes my way." May that prayer be mine if I ever have
cancer, during cancer, and anything else that comes my
way. Let me practice that prayer when all else fails so that
it stills and sustains me.* **Amen.**

We are well when we have faith and trust. Our faith and trust makes us well. You say this over and over, O God, and still we don't hear. Become an echo of wellness deep inside us, O God, and stay there forever. **Amen.**

Help me ask the question Robert Frost asks in his poem, "The Over Bird." Let me ask it repeatedly and not be afraid of it. He asked, "What do we do with a diminished thing?" Let me not be a stranger to diminishment in myself or others. Let me remain curious about what it contains. **Amen.**

Let writing my will be an act of wellness. Let me read my will carefully and slowly as though I really meant it. Let me distribute my jewelry, my collections, and my gathered rocks in a way that helps others remember me with gladness when I am gone. **Amen.**

How deep are the complexities of the everyday?

Of the family, the church, the office, the world?

What the insurance would and wouldn't pay and who fills out what form?

So much happens and most of it we don't even see.

So much is nested within a nest within a nest within yet another nest. Things pile up.

Bring us light to see what is missing and hidden, to see what is neglected, to see what is ignored, both inside us and beyond. Give us light to trustingly see all that is well within us and around us. **Amen.**

Wh-hen we find ourselves feeling guilty that we are sick, blaming ourselves for all that junk food we ate, let us grovel just long enough to be forgiven. Then let us go on, understanding that our health is our responsibility as well as a gift that cannot be controlled. **Amen.**

Some sickness is probably good for us. We don't develop strong spiritual muscles without a difficulty or two. We do the heavy lifting that is necessary to become strong. We de-sentimentalize. On the first day of trouble, we rarely have a smidgen of the spiritual strength we are going to need to get through. The resources do come, the same way fur comes to rabbits by winter. Before winter, they don't have the fur. They get it as the cold grows around them. Keep the alarms going off inside us and let us trust our fur to grow. **Amen.**

When our bodies fail us, O God, remind us of their importance. When our bodies delight us, O God, remind us of their importance. **Amen.**

Whenever my feet leave the ground, bring me back to earth and flesh, my magnificent home.

Help me know, Great Gift Giver, how to understand this elegant universe, with its quacks and its jaguars, its Lexus and olive trees, its ten or eleven dimensions, its wriggling strings, its deep black notes, and membranes, where waves act as particles and particles as waves. Help me understand why the margins cleared for her and not for me or how loose radicals became cancer in him but not in me. Help me understand your majesty and why you think people who have fished all night and caught nothing can still learn to fish. Help me understand why you stick with me when and as I so miserably fail you and myself. Give me a new appreciation for medicine and science and chemistry. **Amen.**

I*n the name of Jesus, who worked the edges on behalf of the whole and the holy, I dedicate this day. On this day I am well. I am well. And all is well. And I give great thanks.* **Amen.**

B*ring me to understand Pascal's Famous Wager. Pascal decided to believe in you, O God, because he thought that even if you don't exist, it is equally possible that you do exist. Why not take the bet on faith? As I go through this healing time, I don't really know what all I believe or don't believe. I don't really know which part, if any, I play in the great Risen Body of Christ. I don't really know my true vocation or what I'm supposed to do today. But I am a person willing to take a chance: I take my chance on you. Assign me a part; give me a role. Let me play it with vigor. If I am having a hard time knowing trust as wellness, give me a little push, a little Pascalian push. Push me to look at what the alternatives are. And then let me take a leap of faith.* **Amen.**

There will be days when we won't be able to be well. You assure us that the darkness is a place for germination. Let us be comfortable in the dark and refuse to put up the sign on our door that we are "Closed after Dark." Let us learn to love night thoughts the way we love stars. Come to us when we think we have been abandoned. Show us how the seeds germinate, and return us from doubt to faith, despair to hope, and sickness to wellness. **Amen.**

No one can teach us how to be sick. Experience is something we don't get until just after we need it. Give us the experience we need when we need it. Give us the know-how we need when we need it. Keep us from making the same mistake more than three times—and transfigure us into people who don't throw away experience so much as use it. **Amen.**

Release us from the confederacy of the mind that issues in internal exile. Bring us out of our places of hiding and fear into the great light of day.

Let us be the people who do know what we have when we have it. Let us not be the other kind of people, those who don't know what they have when we have it.

If we have to depend on others, let us do so with delicacy. Let us neither over-thank nor under-thank but surely thank. Let us be less worried about how we are ever going to repay them for the bedpan or the glass of water and more worried about our recognition of their gift in the moment it is given. **Amen.**

When life is too hard for us and decisions too full of risk, help us to refuse to "take a Pilate." Keep the basin of water away from us. Let us be the people who don't walk away, don't wash our hands, aren't afraid of life and its complexity. **Amen.**

Bend us toward a new week and a new time, O God. As we rise like the sun and set like the sun, admonish us to attend to beauty, to sights and sounds and smells. Let us imagine a long life of wellness, one in which week follows week and wellness follows and deepens wellness. **Amen.**

When we pray for the sick and dying, the doubting and the fallen, may we mean it. **Amen.**

Please give me a ready response when people say I should be more "positive." "Smile," they say, as though it were easy. Make sure my smile comes from the other side of knowing evil's name. Let me not be foolish. Let me be acquainted with sin—and smile because I know about Jesus. **Amen.**

Holy Spirit, you are a kind of dailiness that makes the ordinary extraordinary. You are the reason we may dare to be well. May you find a miracle made in you and of you. Let the miracle be less a cure than a resounding return of trust and faith in all that is. **Amen.**

E. B. White found his wife, Katherine, in the last year of her life, dressed in her business suit, placing daffodils and tulips gently into the Maine ground in November. She was "calmly plotting the resurrection," according to White. Let us calmly plot the resurrection, one bulb and one day at a time. **Amen.**

Teach me not to be afraid of the sick and to be a good caretaker, the kind that knows how to send cards, make phone calls, offer a smile or a removal of the dead amaryllis from the shelf. And let me befriend the practical, the form filled out, the 800 number called, the doctor questioned, the nurse befriended. **Amen.**

F*or the Past not to return, O God, and help me this day to conquer my fears of recurrence,* **Amen.**

O *God, work with me on my attitude about the doctor. Help me not to hate the waiting room so much that it clogs my brain or offends my sense of aesthetics. Help me be patient with the wait. Let me not "go off" about insurance questions or the repeated repeating of the repeat forms. Let me remember I am here for healing and for help. Remove the clutter, both the medical clutter and my clutter, and whatever blocks the healing path.* **Amen.**

W*hen the chaplain calls, let me receive the care he is trying to give. Let me hear the prayer she makes.* **Amen.**

Let me be the one in the waiting room who smiles at other people. Let me be the patient on the ward whom the nurses remember as knowing they exist. Let me receive all the care I need and they want to give and not go overboard on the giving—but also let there be a little give in my get, a certain kindness to the sheet changer, bowl changer, food bringer, and form filler-outer. **Amen.**

When I hear the alarm go off, help me to understand that it may or may not be for me or the one I am visiting. Help me to resist the noise that surrounds in the hospital room. Let me befriend the person I came to see and eliminate the rest of the action. **Amen.**

Thank you for the caretakers who are on their 315th day and don't know how they will go on. Let me be a giver of respite, casually and surely. Let me just show up, every now and then, and take it from there. **Amen.**

When I demand another rainbow and one doesn't come, remind me that there are rainbows in some sky today. Let me enjoy them vicariously. **Amen.**

CHAPTER EIGHT

For That Which Is Other to Us

PRAYER IS NOT PITY. Prayer is a reach for the other, from the other.

Robert called me late on a Friday afternoon. He started by apologizing. He said he was sorry for calling and told me that he had never asked anyone for help before. I hear this all the time, actually. "I've never had to ask for help before. Usually *I'm* the one giving."

The main help I can give Robert is to pray for him, as him, as one who is also stuck in the helping game.

My wonderful and conceited congregation used to use the slogan, "Judson Church is not for the people who are here. It is for the people who aren't here." I beg to differ. Judson is for the people here and the people not here. Both, not either. We spend a lot of time unpacking that suitcase of self and other, host and guest, helper and helpee at Judson. It is good for us.

Prayer permits us to open our suitcases and get over otherizing. Unpacking this kind of suitcase is often very uncomfortable. You find that you have been carrying around a lot of stuff that really doesn't fit. It's like arriving in Miami and finding you have no short sleeve shirts. You have come to life unprepared for life. Prayer prepares us for life. It puts on the right clothes.

Back to Judson. I can't believe the number of people who come to visit me and say, "I know you have better things to do with your time than to bother with me. But..." and then comes the emptied suitcase. There is a deep shaming in our culture about human need. We are not supposed to have it, any kind of it, and if we do, it must be our fault. Or we need to pay somebody to be fixed. Or at least pay it forward.

How many times have you said, "I know I am a lot better off than others"? That is an anti-sacramental point of view. It is like the foot saying to the hand, I don't need you. Or if I do need you, or have any needs, I must be a part of the human race and who wants that? When we pray for others, our first task is to avoid the paternalizing or the patting or the shaming as part of our prayer.

What the poor need is to be relieved of being responsible for their poverty. What the rich need is to be relieved of being responsible for their wealth. Neither deserves either. Or as my brother just said to my nephew in response to him spending a sizable amount on a diamond engagement ring because his bride "deserves it": "Nobody deserves anything."

We desecrate need, regularly. We think our job is to "help" or "fix" or otherwise otherize those in shameful need. The poor are not responsible for their poverty. What the poor want—ask any gang member—is respect. The beatitudes tell us that there is blessing in suffering and that you probably can't be blessed if you can't suffer. People who try to "do something about poverty" are otherizing their own suffering and thereby refusing a blessing. Prayer can help you really do something about poverty by identifying your own poverty.

Prayer helps us suffer and in that suffering to receive a blessing. Not to give one but to receive one. Suffering is knowing the great incompleteness of the one world, that is not fulfilled or complete until everybody gets food and where no one is embarrassed by their wealth or their poverty, whether it be psychological or spiritual or economic in nature. If you want to insist on being ashamed or having shame, go for it. But have the shame for the broken body, the world that does not yet exist. Don't say you belong to a church that exists for others and not for yourself. Better put, we all exist for the whole body, which includes us. What is the blessing? It is mutual respect for those who are "weak" and those who are "strong," and even those who are conceited about how strong they are.

Prayer often caresses what Dr. King meant by the beloved community. He meant a wholeness, a completeness, a fullness of being. He meant a place where my sorry behind can coexist with your sorry behind. In the name of our sorry behinds—that which we try unsuccessfully to put behind us—let us rename the beloved community as something in which we dwell. It is not something our prophetic social action behavior DOES to the world. We are not here to fix the world for others. We are here to live in the world as selves, as full-bodied selves, in a broken world, which is longing to be whole, not fixed.

Prayer takes us to grace. When grace really happens, you can't tell the giver from the receiver. Both are so joyful. We are never going to force CEOs to stop making a hundred times what their janitors make. We are going to show them that such behavior de-sacralizes them and desecrates their own organizations. We are going to show them that they go outside the body when they make too much money. We are going to show the joyful way where the giver and the receiver become one. That will take a little meltdown, a little unpacking of our own suitcases, a little shift in how we see ourselves. It will involve a refusal of otherizing, a melting into the self and the plural world.

I know people who are very poor who don't think they are poor. In that understanding of self, they transcend poverty. I remember getting those baskets at Christmas that the richer people in our little congregation gave to the poorer people in our congregation. Some years the arrival of the basket had dignity. Other years it was shaming. It depended on the attitude of the giver toward the one being gifted. I know people who are very rich who don't define themselves by their wealth or what they can do to help others. Prayer acquaints us with wealth and poverty by taking the other out of our own other.

The two most popular sites on the Internet are porn sites (number one) and genealogy (number two). On porn sites, certain parts of the body are overdone. On genealogy sites, people search for their own behinds.

I watched a man try to fit his car into a parking space that was just too small. He managed to bump the car behind his, which had a driver sitting in it. The driver not only beeped one of those big New York beeps but also got out of his car and yelled at the other guy. Behind the already parked car, there were about six feet. God forbid the one driver would move, allowing the other person to park his car. In sacramental theology, we enjoy moving our car to allow space for somebody else's car. We are delighted to be a part of the great parking lot, which is life. As a landlord, we are delighted to rent apartments at fair rates, and as tenants, we are delighted to park in such places. Prayer is not pity. Prayer reaches for the landlord and parks its car in a space making way.

For knowing where I stop and you start, for knowing a gracious boundary between me and you, for more hope that we can connect, no matter how different we are, I pray. Grant me increasing awareness of how much you want to connect to me and I want to connect to you. And relieve me from the prison of selfishness into a broad and spacious identity, one that honors your size as well as mine. **Amen.**

For people who worry about retirement, and whether what they did matters, let them hear these words. Whatever we have failed to accomplish surely is allotted to others. Comfort those of us who are unfinished and who will never be able to finish. **Amen.**

For musicians: O God we praise you for the small and simple things, for music, that pierces the choice of life with joy, for the health at the edge of sickness, for the moment's quiet in the hours of storm, for the few that held when the many broke and ran, for the honest sounds in a city of noise. We praise you for the minor key, for the oblique kindness, the hidden joy. **Amen.**

For funeral directors who dare to face death every day, while the mourners sing their sad song, for the way they order Kleenex in bulk, we give thanks. **Amen.**

For all the small people who should be listened to. What are the lessons that big movies should learn from small ones? What can big universities learn from small ones? What can adults learn from children and teenagers learn from octogenarians? Can you help us name those lessons? **Amen.**

For an Immigrant

He *worked easy 50 hours for the $300 in his pocket.*
On his way home, on Friday night,
Tired but not exhausted,
The thieves chanted "Juanie, Juanie, Juanie,"
And then robbed him as if they had a right to his money.
And his name.
He had no cop, no wife, no country to call.
His children were waiting
at the Western Union in Chiapas.
He trudged to the place he calls home, now exhausted
And insulted.

My country is the thief.
I am a part of the rip off.
First we steal dignity and then we take the money.

His name was Juan. **Amen.**

A Prayer of Thanks for Grand Central Station on Its Centenary

Great Designer, we give you thanks for the Beaux in the Arts, the clock in the center, the station grand and central by design, the tick of the clock rushing us to track 19, leaving no time to buy a Zabar's or an oyster or a slush. We give you thanks for large visas in crowded places, for the way Apple has snuck its logo into a logo free place, causing us to admire that massive energy that made way for trains.

For the 100 years of the grand centralizing station, and all the people we have met under its clock, we give you thanks. So often our prayers are pastel with nature. Today we thank you for the black and grey of industry within industry within industry, for the lanyard of it and the way we coil to make our train and uncoil when we have made it. So many things are made small by what they exclude and separate. Thank you for letting the grand and central Includer continue to gather and connect. Thank you for the grand in the grand. And get us to our next train with time to spare. **Amen.**

We pray for compassion, for empathy, and for hearts to stay open to those in greater need than we are. We pray not to glaze over at another disaster or typhoon or hurricane or shooting. We pray for all those whose lives were ripped away, for all those who have faced rubble with courage, and for all who remain afraid. **Amen.**

For Those Whose Home Is a Nursing Home

Keep me from being afraid of the old and deaf and lame. Keep me deeply in respect for bodies that work and for those that can't any more. Let me visit a nursing home as often as possible, if for no other reason than to say hello to it. And let me have a plan for my time to be at home and in need of nursing. **Amen.**

For the late shift at the nursing home,

The migrant worker, whose pay is delayed,

The immigrant who is a walking ATM, who loses a whole week to a robber and has to stay silent, hidden and angry,

The tired mother who still has to find the shoes before she can put her children to bed,

The father who knows the car is failing but can't bear to tell its truth to a worried family,

The son whose report card is going to be bad,

The daughter whose soccer game is terrible and whose parents can't take the news,

For all people who live in disturbed and deep water, for their fatigue and their persistence through it, we pray.

*We ask for courage, for patience, for trust, for the refusal to substitute addictive calms for the real thing. We ask for permission to see ourselves in each person mentioned here and to identify, relate and touch. **Amen.***

For My Mother

O God, she didn't always understand me and she wasn't always as present as she wanted to be. Her attention was divided and I sometimes longed so much for it that I shut down in maternal need. Open me up to her now and let the two of us learn to say the words "enough" and "thank you" to each other. **Amen.**

More for My Mother

For what she gave me, I give larger thanks, not just to her but also to the universe. She enjoyed me when I was born, she worried about my trick-or-treat outfit, she provided birthday parties, year after year. She put an ad in the local paper when I turned 60. She loved me a lot. Help me return the favor. **Amen.**

For My Father

O God, he wasn't always his best self. He got angry and didn't know how to turn a corner out of it. He worried himself nearly to death about how to provide well for my siblings and me. He was so proud that we went to college, after he reached only the eighth grade. Help me love what he tried to do for me in a way that maximizes its asset and minimizes its liabilities. **Amen.**

More for My Father

When I hit a homerun, he was beside himself with cheer. When the umpire called a basketball foul he didn't think was right, he booed him way too loudly. To say that he was partisan toward me and his other kids is to leave prayer and to go into understatement. Let me feel the power of his partisan love. **Amen.**

A Prayer for Caleb, My First Grandson

(Pray this prayer for your grandchildren, or write your own)

Surprise, O God, with a future for Caleb that we cannot yet imagine. Down the road let us hope that Caleb's own offspring will want to understand what racism is, or what settlements were in Israel, or whether it was really true that women used to do all the housework or child-raising or couldn't be employed as clergy, like Great-Grandma. Hear with us the joy of Caleb's children being blessed with good air, manageable debt, good topsoil, absurd genetic diversity in plant and animal. Let him always sleep when he is drowsy, but let him usually be artistically, politically, psychologically and spiritually awake. Let him refuse domination and enjoy freedom. **Amen.**

For My Grandparents

Shhe was often blue; he was often sneaking cigars in the garage, paying us not to tell. She kept a mustardy egg salad in a jar for our visits as well as frozen Three Musketeers. Help me not forget the details of their lineage to me and help me become a good detail myself in someone else's life. **Amen.**

For Those Who Do Elder Care

Teach me a gratitude for people who do hard things: who throw away adult diapers, who clean up spills, who deal with grumpiness. Teach me to be good at elder care myself. **Amen.**

For Those Who Supervise Me

I don't always think they are right in the choices they make. I don't even always think they are fair. I do think our lives are richly tangled, and I want to be grateful for the tangle and every now and then to get loose of it too. **Amen.**

For Those Who Babysit Other People's Children

Give me a thankful spirit for those who can be trusted with our children. Help me understand how some days they miss their own more than they want to be with mine. Help me see my way to respect the capacities of those who do this work. **Amen.**

For Bus Drivers and Taxi Cab Drivers

Let me imagine what it is like to drive other people around all day long. Let me imagine what it is like not to be tipped or thanked or spoken to. Give me a little generosity of spirit when I have a driver, and let me treat them like they were a human being, skillfully in charge of my safety. *Amen.*

For My Best Friend

Please let him or her know how much I depend on our shared memories, long stories, messy break-ups, job changes, house redecorations, partner downloads. Let me speak this gratitude myself, and let me do it often and well. *Amen.*

A Prayer for the River Near My Home

(with hopes that you will write yours)

For *rivers that start way north and come way south,*

Hear our prayer.

For people who have left the pews yet long for something sacramental.

Hear our river.

For a way to connect ourselves to a place and a time,

Hear our prayer.

O God, add a sacramental dimension to our everyday lives, even if it is nothing more than remembering where we live, at the end of a great ribbon that dumps into the sea and squaring up to it, noticing it and not just seeing it. **Amen.**

O*thers are not just people, O God. They are also places. The coffee shop, the mall, the parking garage, the doctor's office, the dentist's chair. Yes, all these others have people in them but they are also places, all alone after office hours, lights turned off on the big holidays, lots unfilled at 4 a.m. Let us learn to love our places as if they were our friends and teach us to appreciate that they too have another life, one we will never see. **Amen.***

F*or those pictures we took on our last vacation, the time when we were other than our regular selves, we give thanks. Let us learn to love our on time and our off time as equals, even if very different. **Amen.***

For the Russian whose language I will never understand, the Chinatown that has food I don't think I could eat, the man who bows five times a day in prayer, outside the bus on a mat; for the way I seem to others with my pierced ears and down vests, I pray. Let me appreciate how other I am to others in order that I may be surprised by friendship across boundaries. **Amen.**

When we reach out to an other, let us reach with compassion beyond helping, charity beyond conceit, gifting that forgets about getting. When we give back, let us also give forward, allowing great confusion between the giver and the receiver. When we say, "I went on the mission trip to help and discovered that I was the one helped," let us mean it. **Amen.**

CHAPTER NINE

Prayers for Hatching, Matching, and Dispatching

I HAD A COMPLICATED RELATIONSHIP with my father. Many people do. I still loved him very much although very often that love got disguised as anger. It never made it to non-chalance or indifference. It was a passionate if disappointed love. He knew that and I knew that, and every few years we found a way to connect and remove our costumes. One of the things I knew I wanted from my father was a gift, a blessing, something that I knew he also wanted to give me. That's why the car was so important to me.

After he died, I had been so looking forward to getting my father's car. He had died in August at age 72. The year was 1997. I took the train down to North Carolina and was going to drive the car slowly back north to make it my twenty-two-year-old son's first car. It was a sentimental journey, but I was connected to it. The car still had the red soil of the red clay on it. There was something living about my father and his last car. I was inhabiting the comfort of the delivery. But then as I drove up Route 301 and gave myself the gift of the back way, I realized I couldn't really tell where I was. Everything was the same, even back then in 1997. Every corner. Every traffic light. Every strip mall. My eyes began to hurt. My heart hurt. There were no watermelon stands. There were no silly signs advertising "home cookin'." It always amused me that you could go out to eat in a restaurant and get home cooking. The landscape had become one franchise after another after another. Even the motels were indistinguishable.

I couldn't get over my aesthetic distaste. Had I become an elitist? What was I looking for anyway? Was this dissatisfaction somehow another costume about what didn't happen between me and my father, our refrain from blessing each other? Plus, don't franchises give people jobs with benefits? The landscapes of Virginia and the Carolinas, the landscapes I love so much, were still there. But the billboards were gashing the rolling hills with neon knives. I found it very hard to stay focused on the ritual of the car going from grandfather to son by way of me. I felt more than a little discombobulated. And lurking was this great joke that keeps happening in my own family today: "We are a very judgmental family, my son said judgmentally." Ah. Were we trapped in a franchised family as well?

I wonder if prayer can get us through the dis-patterning of our lives, in time and space. I wonder how prayer gets us through the loss of a father. Or the fear that we are repeating his mistakes? By the way he died a terrible death, alone, sad, abandoned. I needed a way to have affection for him. The old car was going to provide that. He would have approved of its delivery. But it wasn't working. The landscape was in the way. Something was warning me that it wasn't just Daddy that was gone.

My eyes were sore, and not just with tears. I know many of these "fast food" places and "fast sleeping" motels are franchised. Real people own them and work them and park their cars outside them for eight or more hours per day. They aren't completely owned by the Great (Corporate) Discomforter. I want to try to like them. I certainly don't want nostalgia, for my father, his car, and the red clay, to get in my way of being a MODERN person.

On the other hand, I need help. I need a window seat on the ride to the future. I need to be comforted by the land and its pattern. I need to know what it is like to move to the head of the line and not have a father any more. I need to ritualize my oldest son's first car in the same way that I ritualized his Bar Mitzvah and his baptism. Yes, he had both. I know the future is not what it used to be and I know I need rituals to get through my days. I also need rituals to get through my deaths, even when it is not me who died. Not to mention my judgments.

In these prayers for the big times, I realize that I didn't find a way to pray on that drive home. I was in fear that my soul was franchised. These prayers are more communal because they address my main work, that of hatching, matching, and dispatching in public. They also acknowledge how much we need prayers to make the drive home. When blight blights our spirits as well as our roads, we can pray for roadside assistance. We can pray to get some help.

Usually when we get to the big occasions in our lives, they pile on to something more, like what we were trying to do anyway, in our regular ordinary lives. These prayers tell about hatching, matching, and dispatching while trying to live an ordinary life in an extraordinary world.

Whether we call it hooking up or dating or seeing someone or going out, whatever it is we call the great mating ritual of our species, whatever we are thinking when we shop for clothes and ask if some part of our anatomy looks big in these jeans—we are people who want each other. We want to be linked, connected, even married. We want to join at the hip with someone—and laugh in great amusement at how God is said to have created Eve from Adam's rib. First we separate, then we unify. We are often amused by our urgency to be together. When we are amazed at a small human in our arms and know that it is ours and we are its, we usually find a way to pray the child into being, to give the child a tribe. And when we die, we usually find a way to let our loved one go back to whatever red clay is on our own tires. We do find ways to ritualize hatching, matching, and dispatching. These prayers are windows on how some people do that. They beg you to find your own way home. They beg you to find ways to connect your father to your son so that you may also connect you to you. They can't be numbered. Nobody knows how many weddings or funerals or Bar Mitzvahs or baptisms they are going to have until they have them.

For Enduring Love

For love that lasts, for humor that bridges, for long days that last into the night, for good vacations, for pillow talk, for time alone that makes us want to be back together, for all that covenant can provide, we pray. Give us the blessing of many anniversaries and even a larger number of good times. Grant joy to the people around us, about us, and let us not be so much a burden to them as a gift. Let what we have together radiate out in a great circle of human community. And if there be children, let them be especially happy on our anniversaries. **Amen.**

A Morning Prayer on the Day of the Wedding Service

I *am nervous, O God…nervous that I am not good enough, nervous that I won't be able to keep my promises much less dress right, speak right, and act right. I am not as much as I want to be for _____. (Speak Partner's name) Maybe I never will be. But _____ loves me anyway, you love me anyway, and I am awake on this day of transformation. Thank you. Thank you. Thank you. And let my nervousness disappear. Let something like calm take its place. Let me get out of my own way and forget about myself in time to be happy, today and all the days to come.* **Amen.**

A Prayer to Open the Service

Holy God, Blessed Spirit, *you whom some call Yahweh, and others Allah, you whom some call Jesus and others Christ, you whom some know as breath or force or Ruach or Adonai, you beyond any human name or cage, you who transcend the cages we place you in, draw near now and bless this time and place. Let the vows that are spoken be real, let the people who hear them renew the promises they too have made. Hold the space for us as a cosmic canopy and let us shiver with the grace of your presence. Open the doors on all the cages everywhere and let your people breathe free, just as you intended. Let the partnership that emerges at the end of this time renew and be new, let the feast that follows be such a sign of your kind of time that we are newly hungry for an end to any kind of smallness and any kind of poverty. And bless the two who make promises. Let them be as light as lace and as strong as wrought iron.*

Thank you for letting us be here, now. **Amen.**

A Benediction, as the Service Closes

Y*ou walked in here as one person, you leave as another. You walked in here as one couple, you leave as another. You are changed. You have joined the magic of covenant to the love you already had. May it continue to change you and may the uncaged God, the free spirit, the holy vows mark your going outs and your coming ins from this day forward, even forevermore.* **Amen.**

A Prayer of Blessing over the Food (At a Wedding Feast)

T*his feast is a sign of your reign, O God. It is a picture of the joy you intend for all people all of the time. Let us raise our glasses first to you and then to each other and let us promise to live in the feast, now and always.* **Amen.**

A Prayer of Blessing on the First Morning
or Alone Time Together as a Married Couple

Before the pictures arrive or the party is cleaned up, before the first cup of coffee or the first regret, let me kiss you and hold you as though I know who you are. Let me be present to you. Keep me from running by the great moments of my life as though they didn't really happen or I wasn't really there. Slow me down and let me walk, again and again, down the aisle, up to the cake, over to someone I don't know. Let me be surprised by what really happened as opposed to what I thought would happen. Let me relish and repeat, rejoice and evaluate, open the many gifts slowly as though each were the only one. Let me light a candle on this first anniversary and each one to come. Let me be a person who collects joy. **Amen.**

At the Time of the First Fight

W*e don't really know why this happened, O God, nor do we want to be right. We want something more than being right. We just want you to return us to our promises and to see how big they are and how small this is. People say you crossed the river Jordan, that you set a rainbow in the sky. They say you took crumbs and fed 5000. You act like there is always enough to go around. Can you make a miracle also out of us?* **Amen.**

At the Time of the Album's Arrival

We are thankful, O God, for the smiles on each face
and the love in each heart. We wonder why we had so
few quiet moments—and we wonder how we could ever
have looked so good. Ritualize the joy in us so that every
year on our anniversary we go back to these pictures and
rejoice. Ritualize our wedding joy so that we find a way
to sneak feast into our ordinary ways of living. Manage
our lives not by the fleeting joy of our big day but by the
ongoing gladness we have in each other. Some people think
nothing is a miracle and others know that everything is a
miracle. Let us be a part of the last group, enchanted by
and with life. Re-enchant us daily with each other and
with life. **Amen.**

At the Birth of a Child

Exhausted by the exhaustion of life's travel through the birth canal, we find ourselves sweaty, giddy, and glad. We are finally amazed about what we knew was happening but couldn't quite imagine: a child is born. We were a biological vessel and now we are a social vessel. Please, please, please, don't let us drop anything. Let us be a good vessel. Please. We are amazed and glad but scared and fragile. Help us. **Amen.**

On the Death of a Child

This we will never understand. We are not meant to be outliving our children. O God, let us take this day by day and not send our life into the same grave of the innocence we have lost. Show us how. We do not know. **Amen.**

On a Birthday

Today is my birthday and I am glad to be born, glad to be alive, still not sure of why I am here, but knowing there is a reason. Link me to my DNA, my particularity, and my point. Surprise me with some part of it all and me all that I don't yet see. When I blow out the candles, let my last year go by and let the new one come in. **Amen.**

For Time to Think on My Birthday

Sabbath me, O God, and bring me to solitude sufficient to my security. Clarify my thoughts and feelings: let me make sense to me again. Let me know what it is that will never be the same. **Amen.**

A Prayer on My Birthday

I *don't know why my genes had to find each other,*
through those parents, at that time. But they did, and here
I am, suspended between enough self-consciousness for a
hundred people and a simultaneous feeling that I am just a
speck. Join my speckness to my consciousness and get me to
the right size, O God, and hear my thanks that I was born.
Amen.

For an Anniversary

W*e have become like the other couples we see, auto-*
matically grabbing each other's hand on the busy street,
remembering who will forget what, knowing where he left
his keys, what will bother her about what the neighbor
said. We know each other well and we pray not to know
each other too well. Let there be lots of security and lots of
surprise between us. **Amen.**

As Death Approaches

W*e know she is close. We know the day is coming soon when she will no longer be with us. Prepare us for a good-bye that makes sense and is real and is not afraid. Let the intensity of these days mark us and deepen the great well of life from which we draw.* **Amen.**

When the Call Comes

W*e knew the call was on its way. We didn't know it would come this way, on this day, and we know we could not have known. Let our first thought be larger than the arrangements and the plane fares. Let our first thoughts be to dive into the new reality. When we say, "I am so sorry," let us mean it.* **Amen.**

When the Death Is Accidental

*A*ll *of a sudden we are so scared. If that could happen to him, it could happen to me. Why him? Why not the other driver? Was he drinking or texting? Was it his fault? Who can know? Why do I insist on controlling what I can't control? Why do I need to know why?*

Help me move out of the land of explanation into the world of terror. Help me plan for the nightmares. Let me ask for help. And let me be able to help all those affected and not just myself. And make sure I don't just help but also alert people that I need help. **Amen.**

When the Death Is Taking Too Long to Come

We are embarrassed to pray this prayer. But it is time for her to go. Can you help, O God? She wants to go. She is ready. I can't care for her anymore and neither can the doctors nor the hospice nurses. Help us make a good crossing, when it is our time as well. And help her now to cross. **Amen.**

When We Wonder About What's After Life

O God, we have such a need to know what we cannot know. Heaven? Hell? Nothing? Or something? Will I come back? Will I be remembered? Will people come to the funeral or read their e-mail instead? Give us time before the big moment of death to think it through long enough and wide enough to have a conjecture. And then let it and us rest. **Amen.**

For the Anniversary of the Death of a Loved One

It can't be a year already, O God. I still think she will walk through the door and this will all be a big mistake, like the time we lost the tickets at the airport and had to fly on different planes. The route has become circuitous not ended. And yet I have made it through all these breakfasts and dinners alone. I can find the road again. Help me to see it. Maybe it is already there. **Amen.**

On the Anniversary of My Remission

Thank God someone else remembered it has been ten years since the mastectomy. Thank God for the mastectomy and the surgeon's skill in repairing the empty place. And thank God for all who are healed in body and soul. Let me take a minute and say, "Phew. That was close." **Amen.**

A Private Prayer Before a Passover Seder

I *send out the invitations, imagine the food, block out the calendar, iron the tablecloth—and yet I don't feel the high spirituality of a great liberation. Instead, I wonder who will insult whom and whether we should start later or earlier or both for different ones. I hear the loud conversation and its buzz, interrupted by the voices reading from a Haggadah. All those other dinners without formal reading! Now this night that is different from all other nights. Make me a little different too. Liberate me from the details on behalf of the deep dimension of the day. Don't pass me by, O God.* **Amen.**

If We Make Easter Eggs

When we decorate our Easter eggs this year, let us not worry about how long they will last uneaten in the refrigerator. Instead, let us worry about the depth of their colors, the excitement of their roundness, the pastel of spring peaking around the corners and up from the ground. Let us forget about the long time they take to boil and color and decorate. Let us rejoice instead in how time consuming Easter eggs are. And when we are fully present to the gleaned goodness of the present time, let us fertilize our future with the power of these eggs. **Amen.**

The Winter Holidays

Let me learn to say Merry Christmas and really mean it. Let me say Happy Hanukah and really mean it. Let me muse on the great mystery of many religions and all the courtesies they require. Let me send Christmas cards without remorse that I have too many friends. And let me not gain too much weight while also feasting. When the light starts to return at the solstice, let it glow in me too. **Amen.**

On the Anniversary of an Accident

The day had started in a regular way and ended without any hope for yesterday being the same as tomorrow. The deer came out of nowhere and hit me and destroyed my new car. There were antlers in the front seat and an air bag's dust everywhere. My son and daughter came to the hospital. They tried to act like they weren't scared. I still have to drive that road and am almost over marking the spot where the ambulance found me. Let me take a minute and say, "Phew. That was close." And thank you for close encounters of a strange kind. Thank you for the reminder about immortality and how it is not mine. **Amen.**

On the Anniversary of Learning to Pray

For a long time, my time was chaotic, belonging to the clock and the appointment and the great ticking, ticking, ticking. Now my time is shared with the one I lean toward, who sometimes is called God and sometimes gets an Amen and sometimes gets the first person and other times the third person. Let my "I" become a "we," over time, O God. Let my life have a sense of Amen. **Amen.**

When Making a Vow to a Roommate or a Friend or a Partner

Your people will be my people. Your neighbor will by my neighbor. Your crazy uncle will be my crazy uncle. Your loud and boisterous family will by my loud and boisterous family. Your problems will be my problems. **Amen.**

CHAPTER TEN

Prayers Through the Months and Seasons

A SEASONED PERSON HAS A SENSE of place in time and a sense of time in place. Prayer seasons us. People used to have spring and fall house cleaning—back when domestic life had a pattern. Now that a lot of time feels the same, almost like it has been homogenized, it is harder to be seasoned. We do put the summer clothes away and get out the sweaters, but we do so without much sense of time and place. Some of us even forget to put the lawnmowers away, long after mowing season is over. They rust. Still others of us haven't changed the filter on our furnaces for a decade. We forget the seasons. Praying through them could help us remember them. The seasons have not forgotten us.

Think of these prayers as a reminder to change your

passwords or to get the car registration done or the battery changed in the smoke alarm before you get burned for not having done so. Don't use the seasons as a stick, one that says you should be better at being seasoned. Instead consider them permission, a permission to have a life that pays attention to the way time changes, leaves fall, filters need refreshing.

The best criticism of what's wrong with us is to practice being better. Just practice. Prayer is the practice of the presence of something or someone like God. That's all it is. "How do you get to Carnegie Hall?" asks the old joke. Practice, practice, practice. I am a card-carrying imperfectionist who practices being seasoned. She does not succeed.

We often say at my under-resourced and over-programmed church that Judson has to learn to pitch high and inside, low and down. If we are going to fight outside of our weight class, then we better refine our methodologies. We often say we need half the programs with double the impact. Our other slogan is that we need "fewer finer." I think a lot of people live lives like Judson lives its ministry. We promise more than we can deliver. Prayer adds energy to the delivery. Seasoned prayers take away that awful question, "Does anybody really know what time it is? Does anybody really care?" It replaces it with a sense that this is January and that is October.

Seasonal change often brings me sleep disruption. I am not alone. When unable to sleep, we can pray for the three months of the season coming or the season just past. This is not counting sheep so much as making connections. When seasons change or sleep gets disrupted, we can also pray for our worries. Son bothering you? Pray for him. Mortgage late? Pray for the bank. Skin infection? Pray about how grateful you are for your skin. Bad haircut? Pray for how good you used to look. Don't think of any topic as too small or too large for prayer. And become aware that the seasons will change. They always do. What is bothering you now won't be bothering you then. (Yes, something new will come to take its place.)

As a child, I used to pray the famous prayer, "Now I lay me down to sleep, I pray the Lord my soul to keep, if I should die before I wake, I pray the Lord my soul to take." If you prayed this prayer as a child, consider how it has changed for you over the seasons of your life. I no longer find it useful. I think God already has my soul and will after I die. I am no longer threatened by dying in my sleep the way this prayer threatened me as a child. I do pray to wake before I die but that is very different. We all like to think that we are like trees, growing rings each year, becoming different although still trunked to the same original kernel.

One more thing about prayer: it is not just for ourselves or to cure our own spiritual or actual insomnia. Prayer is also a way to get out of the solitary confinement of our own bruised spirit. Some seasons we feel strong enough to hand out ten blessings a day and then be off duty. Some seasons we may want to say a *Kaddish* (or mourner's prayer) on the date of every death you remember. The experience of death changes how we understand a season. If she died while it was snowing, snow will always remind us. Some seasons you won't have any death to remember at all. There are years like that, when the grim reaper just doesn't find your address or your calendar. When you pray your prayer of mourning, you might also think of doing it for the spring that is about to pass into summer. You may want to sway your body or bow as some Jews do as you let each season turn into the other. Don't think of the swaying and bowing as a crutch. It is actually an ancient practice of using a motion to help still the body. It is called *davening*, a way to lean in and out of the prayer. You move forward, then backward, in a rhythmic motion. Like a prayer bead or a rosary, crutches are very helpful to people who are injured. They are even helpful to some who are not.

There is a way in which each season beckons its own prayers only to turn us back into a great universality of life. In every season, we can take our heart to the downtrodden and understand the words trodden down. In every season, we can remove our boot. We don't just feed the homeless when it is cold or at Thanksgiving with our leftover cranberry sauce. In every season we can take the pointed finger and unbend it, massaging it as we do so. In every season and any season where we have lost our grip, we can stay away from people who tell us to get a grip. In every season we can pray our way into disability or aging or griplessness. In every season we can listen to God's grant of a grip and God's unintentional removal of same.

I keep pictures of trees on my bulletin board. Fall, summer, winter, spring. They delight me. They help me remember what a friend called the idiosyncratic eloquence of an old apple tree bent out of shape by the fruit it has born. Seasonal prayer allows us both to bend and be bent.

When my second son, a twin, almost died at birth, I had to sing Easter hymns, all verses, to him, as they removed the respiration two months into his life. We didn't know if he would or could breathe on his own. His sister had come out two seconds earlier and she was fine. He was not. The whole ICU liked my weak voice. He survived. Some of their babies didn't. Easter has never been the same for me.

Prayer teaches us that for some people it is uphill both ways.

Prayer allows us to bend toward each other and not be broken. Prayer knows that the way out is the way in. Often a hymn can help open the doors that go into what we call our hearts.

Many therapists talk about the unfreezing stage. By that they mean the moment when personal growth is possible. The anger has begun to melt. The refusal has met its match. The hurt is starting to go away. Something like insight—a truly great word—is coming. Insight means we see in. We see better. We see differently. Prayer is a plea for insight. It is a plea for presence. Prayer helps us be less proud about how humble we are. It changes us. Prayer helps us be where we are when we are there; that practice unfreezes us. I am not arguing that prayer is therapy. It is not. But it is an aid to therapy as strong in force as summer, fall, winter, and spring. Prayer lets us look more than once at the season as its breezes breeze by.

Prayers to Try in January

As the calendar page turns and I seek the capacity to turn myself, let me resolve to imitate a turnaround kind of company. Let me go from strength to strength. Let what I have left undone be relinquished or plowed into a new furrow of hope. Take me beyond New Year's resolutions into New Year's turnings. So that by turning and turning I turn out right. **Amen.**

The sunsets are so early and my days are so long. Let me learn how to maximize the light and minimize my greed for it. **Amen.**

Let me remember the birthdays of those I mark. Let me enter their dates on my clean-slate calendar. Even if I forget to send a card, let me pray when I see their names on their numbered day. **Amen.**

Prayers to Try in February

As my skin gets drier and drier and the days get colder and colder, anoint my head and hands with oil and let my cup overflow. From its overflow, let me anoint others. No one wants a dry spirit. Instead quench me with joy. Let me spread it around. **Amen.**

For that late afternoon light of February, I give thanks. It is so slant, so cornered, so different. Let me treasure it. **Amen.**

For the shortness of this month, let me pray and allow me to muse on how short most days and months really are. Let me understand that musing is a winter luxury and enjoy it as much as the birds enjoy the seeds I put in their feeder to get them through to the warmer time. **Amen.**

Prayers to Try in March

Let me find a way to my own Ash Wednesday, even if I don't wear the ashes or marvel at those who do. Let the ashen way prepare me for spring. **Amen.**

Let me find a way to pass over even if I am not Jewish. Let me invite myself to a Seder and understand that Exodus is more than a bible story. Find a place for me that I can leave, intentionally, so that I can be more deeply at home on the globe. **Amen.**

Let me be an Easter aficionado. Let me belt out the Easter hymns as though I mean them. **Amen.**

Prayers to Try in April

When we are gluttonous for spring, let us not hate it but await it. Teach us to love mud, and if not love it, at least understand it. To everything there must be a season, right? Forgive my urgency for spring. **Amen.**

When we put our winter coats away and locate most of the lost mittens, when the hats are safely stored on a shelf, let us be glad for what we have known of cold and ready for warm to replace it. **Amen.**

Help me understand why the poets say April is the cruelest month, and when I am still cold in April, let me learn the patience that nature must have. And if nature shows impatience, let me join it there too. **Amen.**

Prayers to Try in May

Let May be springtime in our hearts, with blossoms that are breathtaking both internally and externally. Let us be lusty for planting and caress our seed packages every day till the earth warms up enough to receive them. Let Memorial Day come with our picnic already prepared. **Amen.**

For graduations and end of school year celebrations, we give thanks. Graduate our spirit from one level of learning to another, no matter how long gone we have been from school. Commence in us a new thought. Let graduation not be a one-time thing but something that happens over and over as each year of learning ends, like the rings that surround and age the trees. **Amen.**

Find me in the woods looking for rare flowers, the ones that have the courage of spring and the shortest of moments in bloom. Engage me in an appreciation for the rare in myself and in the woods. **Amen.**

Prayers to Try in June

Help us not to listen to the people who say summer ain't what it used to be. Help us to defy them, to eat out at night or to build a fire in the back yard or to lie down in the grass and catch the stars. Don't let the doomsayers have their way with us. Help us counter the gloom of global warming with a hope that blocks its scorching way with us. Let us know global scorching and also love what summer is so much that we stop it. **Amen.**

Did you really make June bugs? Do they really have a purpose or are they just here for us to enjoy? **Amen.**

Let me plant a garden, or at least one seed, the kind that will take ninety days to grow and become a pumpkin, or just thirty days to become a salad. Let me be a planter first and a harvester later. **Amen.**

Prayers to Try in July

Give us thanks for our country and let a fireworks display touch our patriotic hearts and give them light and sound and voice. **Amen.**

Send us swimming, O God, or at least floating, or at least help us to get wet. Help us forget what we look like in a bathing suit or at least forget long enough to lie out in the sun in public. When we float, let us be glad that something holds us up, all the time, and not just in the water. **Amen.**

When it is time to turn on the air conditioner, let us make a ritual out of the internal weather. Let us be grateful for climate control, as we fear climate change. Let us say a little prayer for electricity and refrigerator and the awesome power we have to change the temperature. **Amen.**

Prayers to Try in August

If we are lucky enough to have a vacation, let us appreciate it. Let us turn off our computers and hide our cell phones, except for fun. Let the office have a vacation from us. It probably needs it more than we do. **Amen.**

Let us know the meanings of the words *time off,* and forgive our compulsivity to be on all the time. **Amen.**

If the stores start advertising back-to-school sales too soon, help us understand our economy and how it is almost like that song, "Turn, turn, turn." Let us turn with grace but also hang on to warm summer nights as though they really mattered. **Amen.**

Prayers to Try in September

Seasons change, and so do we. How are we different than we were in the spring? If we haven't changed, why not? If we have changed, is it for the better or are we just sinking into something? Let us name our season, even if it has the name fall. **Amen.**

For the apple's crispness and the corn's sweetness, the sneaky turn to red from green in the leaf, for the new potato and the one left over from last year, we give you thanks. Help us to appreciate the earth and how it never stops turning. **Amen.**

For our bicycles and backpacks, our readiness to learn again, for children's nervousness about their new classmates and new teacher, for notebooks and schoolbooks, hear our thanks. **Amen.**

Prayers to Try in October

Daylight savings time is coming to add an hour to our morning and steal an hour from our evening. We can fall back and get the extra hour the globe stole from us in spring. Let us enjoy that extra hour, as though we really understood how time works and when the sun properly ought to rise and set. **Amen.**

For the first frost, we give thanks. Hoary or full, let it dazzle us with its brightness and its sure-footed march in time. **Amen.**

Find us a calendar that lasts forever, and let us mark it with the full harvest moon. Help us remember where we were last year when its great roundness pierced the horizon, and help us imagine where we will be next year. Put the moon in our context and us in its. **Amen.**

Prayers to Try in November

O God, when November scares us in a shudder of cold wind or a missing scarf or only one glove available, and when we see that we should have packed up last winter more carefully since we knew this one was coming, plant our feet firmly on the hard ground and let us remember that for everything there is a season. **Amen.**

Hasten the day when everyone in the world will eat as well as we will on Thanksgiving. **Amen.**

When we sing "Harvest Home" this year, let us imagine our harvests coming home, our legacies being lived, our loved ones remembering us as fruit and grain, well harvested. **Amen.**

Prayers to Try in December

As we close this year of learning to pray, may we remind ourselves of all the rules that are golden: that we not treat others the way we didn't want to be treated. That we never impose on others what we would not choose ourselves, as Confucius puts it. That we "regard your neighbor's gain as yours and your neighbors loss as yours," as Lao Tzu puts it. And never let us forget good old Seneca, "Expect from others what you did to them." Permit prayer to make us a tad bit wiser, and if not that, then at least to know what rules are golden. **Amen.**

Energy and Spirit, please amuse us today so that we may amuse others. Let us laugh at least once an hour or at least giggle. **Amen.**

As the gift-wrapping paper comes out of the place where it has hidden, let gift giving gladden our spirits almost as much as the gifts we receive will do the same. **Amen.**

A Prayer at the End of One Year and the Beginning of Another

Great originator, you who are the true original, you whom we can only copy over and over again, draw near and humor us while we tell you what little truth we know. Remind us that nobody ever really discovers anything, that we are all rich remnants, all lame, all exiled, and also all gathered together. Remind us that it is you who first lifted the eyelids on the universe and you, you who will gently lower them when the time is right. Strangers here, heaven are our origin and our destiny. Draw us therefore to surface and depth, style and substance, to habitats full of communion where we can also stare into space alone. Let us know our street corner and your galaxy, both, not either. Stop the fighting we do over time and space, land and landscape. If you can't stop it, help us to refuse to participate for at least today.

Remind us in the Jesus way that every collapse contains within it a reconstruction.

Teach us the arts of interior decoration, remodeling, how to renovate after storms damage. Teach us new ways to inhabit your land and your canopy of stars.

Let us walk the route of tears, over and over again, with heads lifted high, whether they are the route of the Boston Marathon or the Vietnamese War, the path of Two Row Wampum or the road up to Golgotha. As we walk these roads of tears, let us imagine what you are up to next and help us to discover it and it alone. **Amen.**

Where to Start:
On Writing Your Own Prayers

EVERYONE CAN WRITE PRAYERS. A prayer notices where we are now and then imagines that we have a destination. A prayer is alertness to the present and pointing to the future that is deep within it.

We write prayers by paying extra attention to our ordinary experience, choosing what of it matters most to us, writing it down, editing ourselves, and ritualizing the saying of what we have written. It sounds complicated at first glance but it is not. When we pay attention to our ordinary experience, we are mini-novelists, taking the ordinary steps of each long day and resolving their direction and destination. Many say that a good novel is one where we turn the pages actively, where we side first with one character, then another, and back to the other, understanding every challenge that each character faces and every gift that each has. A good novel doesn't allow us to take sides but instead helps us identify with the hero and the villain simultaneously.

Like good novelists, when we pray, we choose what of the thousand things that happen is most important. We pay attention and we choose. Then we journal or write down what happened. Then we reflect and edit the language we use to describe what we have chosen to attend. We choose the details that show character, create suspense, and add value to the events that swirl all around us. We become more connected to our own internal villain and our own internal hero. Finally we say our prayer.

Some prayers are laments. They know that what we hope for may not become real. They may be a form of anticipatory grief. Others are gratitude, noticing the June bugs when the June bugs are there. Still others are confessions, wishing that we could be more and pointing us to a turning, even repentance. Most prayers are some combination of thanks, lament and turning.

Some call a prayer the reflection that is embedded in action—or in short hand action-reflection and the unification of these two so often thrown apart. Most of us act and act and act and forget to think and think and think about our acting, acting, acting. Most of us are pause deficient, and a prayer is just a pause to collect experience. Today the experience may be haste and rushed, packed and filled; there may be no margin to our day. Tomorrow may be clear and uncluttered, open and spacious. These words that describe the day and its differences can end up in a one-sentence prayer. "Today may be rotten and a facsimile of living but tomorrow I will digest all that came at me and from me today."

The first step in writing a prayer is to pay attention. Yes, there are simultaneous first steps involved. We multitask the writing of prayer, paying attention to what is in front of us as well as what God might be in the midst of it. We are beginning a dialogue with God. Why not let God know where we are and what we are experiencing? Why not imagine a reader who wants to read our lives along with us?

The second step, after paying attention and enjoying the luxury of giving our own lived experience a proper look from a godly perspective, is to choose what matters. What matters on a cluttered day? What matters on a clear day? Are we to "see forever" on the clear day and just survive on the cluttered one? If we were having a good conversation with a good friend, what form would that conversation take? Thanksgiving?

Rescue? Change? Transformation? Salvation? You could pray this simply: "From haste and its waste, rescue me, O God." Or use these words, "For open space and a sense of being clear, hear my thanks, O God."

Note the verbs. They activate the conversation. They open up the conversation. They are the destination or what we want or where we are aiming part of the prayer. I can imagine a good prayer just noting that we are in a chaotic way on a chaotic day. I can imagine just experiencing the chaos. What I can't imagine is wanting that experience to continue. Nor can I imagine having a wonderful experience and not wanting to send a thank-you note.

When I suggest the third step of writing down the chosen focus and experience, I do so as a way to prepare to edit. Writing something down makes it real. Of course we can pray the kinds of prayers that are too deep for words or even sighs. Often the most praying we do is contained in the phrase, "OMG" or "Oh, my God." We say that when we hear that a train has left the track and killed a baby. "Oh, my God." That is an inarticulate prayer. It is a good prayer. But better prayers, more disciplined praying require a little more reflection. We get to ask the questions, *What does this mean? Why am I in chaos again today? Have I stopped to enjoy this clear day?*

Paying attention, choosing the transformation that matters, writing down what we have understood as our experience, leads directly to the poetry of the prayer. When we write it down, we can edit it.

"From haste and its waste, rescue me, O God." Why the word *rescue*? Why not the word *save*? Why not a less common prayerful concept, like "let me escape." Or "give me a detective's brain so I can find my way out of this ordinary mess." Why not start with the verb? Save us from haste and its waste. Or why not reverse field? Let me engage the haste of this day so that it not be waste but instead muscle training for the next multi-tasking moment I face. Why not go in rather than out? Why not go inward rather than outward as a way to experience our lives? Our reflex in today's culture is outward: fix it, work harder, do more, etc. Inward is the place of energy for the outward. Prayer reverses the outward motion just long enough to allow us to go out with Spirit. Go toward the vortex of the tension, the way a canoeist rides the waves. Take something bad and give thanks for it as a preparation for learning from it.

Editing a prayer is not just editing language. It is also editing the concept. What is it we really want? Good friends don't just give us what we think we want; they help us to see what we need. "Oh, God, show me why I hurry. What am I trying to prove?" Is the point of our life just to be still standing when the music stops?

I asked a man who seemed very happy to explain himself to me. He said, "I am open to people, open to God. I'm not really much at all." It sounded like a prayer to me. I prayed later that day, "Let me be open to people and open to God, let me stop trying so hard to be anything more." Editing our desires after we have written them down can re-sacralize what we have de-sacralized.

After we have written a short prayer and edited it, we are ready to "pray" it. We are ready to say it. Some prayers need constant repetition, like the "Our Father" or the Twenty-Third Psalm. There is nothing wrong with the good old oft-repeated prayers. They are in fact stunning as trail markers on our way to spirituality. Here I have focused on more custom designed personal prayers. These are *sui generis*; they are from today's focus and for today.

From attend to choose to write to edit to repeat: that is the process of common people writing common prayers for themselves as a spiritual exercise. It is also the process many of the great writers of prayers use. Think of it as the five point guide to writing common prayers for common people. You will notice this little guide showing up in many famous prayers. First attention, then choosing, then writing, then editing, then re-peating: it is all really a flow to focus, and the flowing focus is what we call prayer.

Not all of us can pray briefly. Brevity is an art. The trick is in the editing and in letting go of all that is unnecessary. Like the great sculptors, our "small" prayers come from taking away all the clay that is of no use. Writing shorter is much harder than writing easier. Likewise public speaking. Short and brief are not just bulleting or shortening. They are the stock in the soup, the density of the day. They are the simmered down.

One of the great things about praying is that there is no need to become famous or even good at it. Prayer is not a place to succeed or show off. Prayer is a perfect practice for imper-fectionists. Perfectionists will have a little trouble praying. (I like this sentence.) Prayer is pause, pause to collect yourself and to see more deeply who you are, where you are from, and where you are going. "God, grant me the power to become myself, over time. Amen."